Happy Mothers Day
Love, Renice

A CUP OF COMFORT®

for
Mothers and Daughters

Stories that
celebrate a very
special bond

Edited by Colleen Sell

Aadamsmedia

Avon, Massachusetts

For my grandmother, Mary; my mother, Jeannie;
my daughters, Jennifer and Christine; and my granddaughter, Brianna:
May our circle of light, laughter, and love be forever unbroken.

Published by
Adams Media, an F+W Publications Company
57 Littlefield Street, Avon, MA 02322 U.S.A.
www.adamsmedia.com and *www.cupofcomfort.com*
ISBN 10: 1-59869-661-0
ISBN 13: 978-1-59869-661-5

Printed in the United States of America.

J I H G F E D C B A

Library of Congress Cataloging-in-Publication Data
A cup of comfort for mothers & daughters: stories that
celebrate a very special bond / edited by Colleen Sell.
p.   cm.
1. Women—Religious life. I. Sell, Colleen.
HQ755.85.C856 2003
306.874'3--dc21
2002155579

This publication is designed to provide accurate and authoritative information
with regard to the subject matter covered. It is sold with the understanding that
the publisher is not engaged in rendering legal, accounting, or other professional
advice. If legal advice or other expert assistance is required, the services of a
competent professional person should be sought.
—From a *Declaration of Principles* jointly adopted by
a Committee of the American Bar Association and
a Committee of Publishers and Associations

Many of the designations used by manufacturers and sellers to distinguish
their products are claimed as trademarks. Where those designations appear in
this book and Adams Media was aware of a trademark claim, the designations
have been printed with initial capital letters.

This book is available at quantity discounts for bulk purchases.
For information, please call 1-800-289-0963.

Acknowledgments

When I first started gathering stories for the flagship book in the Cup of Comfort series, my objective had been simple: to do a good job. In my mind, that meant compiling a cohesive collection of engaging stories that would lift readers' spirits and bring hope to their hearts. I believed then, as I do now, that sharing our personal stories benefits not only the listener, but also the storyteller. I knew the job would be challenging and hoped it would be rewarding. What I didn't realize was just how challenging it would be, and how much hard work by so many other people it would require. Nor could I have imagined how rewarding this experience would be, how much healing and joy it would bring to me personally.

In fact, at the time *A Cup of Comfort* was launched, for the first time in my life, I felt utterly hopeless and joyless, and nothing seemed to comfort me. My son, the youngest of my three children, had been suffering from a debilitating brain injury for almost five years. Recovery had become increasingly less likely; survival was iffy. So I did what I had to do: I did everything I could to help my son, and I got up every morning and went to work.

But then a remarkable thing happened. My work—thanks to the countless good people who sent in stories that have so touched and inspired me, and thanks to the amazing staff at Adams Media whose incredible support makes it all possible, and thanks to the readers who've embraced these wonderful books—helped me to heal, and to feel joy again, and to celebrate life's blessings.

And for that, I am most grateful.

A deep bow of appreciation goes to the authors whose stories are featured in *A Cup of Comfort for Mothers & Daughters* and to Kate Epstein, Laura MacLaughlin, Kate McBride, Betty Eastman, Mary Hanley, Sandy Smith, Sue Beale, Sophie Cathro, Gene Molter, and Bob Adams.

Thanks also go to my husband, for putting up with my long hours at work and away from us; to my lovely mother and daughters, for their brilliant presence in my life; and to my son, whose journey back to wellness never ceases to amaze and inspire me.

Contents

Introduction

"I love you the more in that I believe you have liked me for my own sake and nothing else."

~John Keats

I have two daughters, one granddaughter (so far), two sisters, and one (only one) mother. My mom is the only child of an essentially only child. Among all those mother-daughter combinations, no two relationships are alike. Some are complex, sometimes difficult; others are simpler, easier, and usually enjoyable. None are superficial. All are deep and enduring, forged soul to soul with abiding love.

Although our relationships with our fathers and sons are equally significant to us, there is something unique, almost magical, about the mother-daughter connections in my family. When one of my daughters calls unexpectedly, I know which one it is before I pick up the phone, and I know at the sound of her "Hi, Mom" whether she's calling with good news, for comfort, or just to touch base. The same thing happens when my mom calls me, and in reverse when I call her or my daughters. (This mother-daughter telepathy kind of spooks the male members of our family.)

Regardless of where we are in our respective lives, the mothers and daughters in my family stay connected and try, at least, to stay tuned in to one another. We have an impact on and have left an imprint on one another's lives. And while things between us aren't always warm and fuzzy, we are—contrary to the popular belief about mother-daughter relationships—close friends who applaud one another's accomplishments, lean on each other, and have loads of fun together.

We are not alone.

If you'll excuse me while I put on my journalist's hat, research has shown that, contrary to all the negative jibe and jokes about the supposedly sorry state of mother-daughter relationships, 70 to 90 percent (depending on the study) of adult women report having positive, flourishing relationships with their mothers and daughters. Many middle-aged women cite their mothers and daughters as their "best friends." Apparently, most of us have to make it over what my grandmother called "fool's hill," the adolescent and young adult years when you're trying to simultaneously pull away from and prove yourself to your mother, before we can put down our guards and really let our moms into our hearts. There are, of course, fractured and dysfunctional mother-daughter relationships that require more than maturity and time to repair or reconcile.

The amazing thing is, the bond between mothers and daughters nearly always remains intact through thick and thin, despite differences and disagreements and distance, and over time. Their consistent love and devotion to one another is even more amazing. What other relationship is that resilient and unconditional? And what could be more comforting than to know that from the moment you are born to your mother and from the moment you give birth to your daughter you are loved by someone with whom you share a sacred link that is carried, like DNA, from mother to daughter, generation after generation?

When I was growing up and misbehaved, my mother would often say that though she didn't like what I'd done, she always loved me. I used the same line on my daughters, who would either cry from hurt feelings over Mommy being "mad" at them, or pout and tell me I was a "mean mommy"—that is, until they were about twelve, after which they would sass that it was impossible to love someone and hate what they did at the same time. On my last visit to my older daughter's home, I overheard her reprimanding her six-year-old daughter in the next room, saying that she loved her, but didn't like it at all when she screamed at her big brother. My granddaughter gasped, ran into the living room, threw herself in my lap, and with tears in her eyes said, "Mommy's mad at me, Grammie Nut! She's meeeaan!" I smoothed her hair away from her chipmunk cheeks, dabbed her tears away with her butterfly hankie, kissed her forehead, and said, "Ah, sweetie, I know. That's because she had a mean mommy who loves her very much, too."

Oh, that all the misunderstandings and mistakes and mysteries between mothers and daughters were so easily resolved. The important thing to remember is, most *can* be resolved—even if the resolution comes only from accepting one another, as is, warts and tantrums and "mean mommy" and all. The rewards of a loving mother-daughter relationship are well worth any effort it might require, and they far outweigh and outlast any "troubles" that may arise.

Surely, the unique relationship shared by mothers and daughters is one of life's most fascinating and profound blessings. In *A Cup of Comfort for Mothers & Daughters*, you'll find a rich and varied collection of inspiring and uplifting true stories that celebrate this very special bond. My wish for you, dear reader, is that these slice-of-life tales inspire you to cherish and enjoy even more, and to heal and strengthen, if need be, your relationship with your mother and, if you are so fortunate, your daughter(s).

—*Colleen Sell*

 # Time Out

I flung aside the covers and bolted upright, wide-eyed. "Wake up!" I shook Mike's shoulder gently, then harder. "We overslept!"

I raced to the girls' room, frantic and smelling of morning breath, pulled the two older ones out of the bunk bed and led them to the bathroom with their eyes closed. Trusting that they could walk through the morning routine in their sleep, I pulled open drawers and laid out their clothes, while the baby slept on in her crib. Then I sped down the hall, pulling open the bathroom door in transit. "Your clothes are on the bed! Dress fast; we're really late!"

"Can we have pancakes today, Mommy?"

"No! Daddy will butter some toast for you to take out the door. Hurry!"

I threw on a pair of yellow slacks and a matching T-shirt. Dress at the school where I taught was casual. Permanent press, great! No time for ironing. No time for a shower, either. I ran a brush through my hair and while I dashed on a little makeup, I listened to the girls in the next room.

"I hate these overalls."

"Me, too. I wish Mom didn't know how to sew."

"Me, too. I wanna wear a pretty dress."

"I wanna wear my orange T-shirt with the sparkles and my jeans with the silver studs."

"Can you reach my pink dress?"

"Sure. Will you pull out my T-shirt? It's under your bed."

Ordinarily I would have intervened and ensured they wore appropriate and clean clothing, but under the circumstances I decided to prioritize and let it go. Five minutes later we convened at the front door. Mike handed out lunch boxes and toast to go, and we were off and running!

Sasha looked up at me as we left our building. "You look pretty, Mommy. I like yellow."

"Let's walk a little faster," I replied. What a sight we were—the harried, wild-eyed mom with a book bag slung over one shoulder, herding two tousled little girls who had forgotten to brush their hair but were dressed to kill, one in sequins and studs, the other in ruffles. We navigated a long city block with commendable speed, darting around slower pedestrians and speaking as little as possible except for an occasional "hurry up." Amazingly, we were only a few minutes behind schedule. If we kept up a brisk pace, I thought, I'd be able to drop them at their elementary school in ten minutes and sprint to my own school in time to clock in at 8:30—with a little luck.

It didn't happen. As we approached the first intersection, the light changed and we had to stop. Now, if you've ever been in New York, you know that nobody actually waits for the pedestrian walk signal before crossing. Savvy pedestrians watch the opposite traffic signal and step off the curb when it turns yellow, look both ways, and start walking when it turns red. The pedestrian walk sign comes on when you're about halfway across. I stepped off the curb, looked left and right, and jumped back as a bus beat the light. Though I'd given myself plenty of room and was in no danger of losing my life or incurring bodily harm, I hadn't seen the mud puddle.

"Oh, no!" So much for the split-second timing that had gotten us out the door almost on time. I stared down at my slacks, splattered with dark mud spots from waist to cuffs, doing lightning calculations of how many minutes it would take to dash back home and change, weighing that against the pros and cons of just going to work as I was.

Suddenly, Sasha's head disappeared from my peripheral vision. I whirled around to see her sitting on the sidewalk, opening her lunch box, and I blew up. "You know we're running late, and you saw what just happened, and all you can think of is you want a *snack!* What's the matter with you?"

Her bottom lip quivered. Great, I thought. On top of everything else, she was going to start crying right here on the street.

Big brown eyes looked up at me and brimmed over. "I was just getting you a napkin so you could clean your pants."

My frustrations melted along with my heart as I knelt down to hug her. Suni put a comforting hand on my shoulder. Droves of commuters skirted around us, a little island in the rush-hour hustle, and when the light turned red again, we were still in a huddle.

"Mom . . . I have an idea." Suni usually did. Her ideas matched her favorite clothes—neon with lots of glitter. "Let's not go to school. Let's all call up and say we have a cold. Actually, I think I do, a little." She coughed. "And Sheila can stay home from the baby-sitter's . . . and Daddy can make us all pancakes."

"Blueberry!" That was Sasha's idea of heaven on earth.

"And then we could spread a blanket on the floor and play Chutes and Ladders." Suni was on a roll, and she knew it.

My priorities took a new turn, for the better, I think. What would I actually lose if I took a day off? And how much more would I gain? We threw our half-eaten cold toast in a trashcan and ran laughing hand in hand back to our building, conspirators in a grand plot. The blueberry pancakes were the best we'd ever had, and we played Chutes and Ladders until everybody won at least once.

The mud spots came out in the wash. Most bad things do; life is like that. I'm happy to say that, after being mentored by a sweet little girl sitting on the sidewalk getting a napkin out of her lunch box, my priorities remained firm: Punctuality is important, but not as important as your family.

One of my girls called me the other day. Married just one year, she and her husband had called in sick and spent the day together. They didn't play Chutes and Ladders, but from the sound of her voice, I gathered that whatever they'd done, they'd both won! She's going to be a good mother.

—Nancy Massand

She Left a Mess Behind

I watch her back her new truck out of the driveway. The pickup is too large, too expensive. She'd refused to consider a practical compact car that gets good gas mileage and is easy to park. It's because of me, I think. She bought it to spite me.

She'd dropped out of college, and I'd made her come home. All summer long she'd been an unstable cloud of gasoline fumes, looking for a match to set her off. We'd fought about her job, about leaving school, about her boyfriend and her future. She'd cried a lot and rebuffed all my attempts to comfort her.

"I'm twenty, almost," she'd told me so often my teeth ached. "I am an adult!"

Each time I silently replied, No, you are not. You still watch cartoons, and expect me to do your laundry, and ask me to pick up toothpaste for you when I go to the grocery store.

Now she is gone, off to be an adult far away from me. I'm glad she's gone. She's impossible and cranky and difficult to get along with. I am sick of fighting, tired of her tantrums.

Her father is angry. He watches television and will not speak. He helped her with the down payment on the truck and got her a good deal. He slipped her cash before she left. I want to say, If only you hadn't helped her buy the truck, she would still be here. It's a lie.

"I am never coming back," she told me. "I'm a grown-up now. I want to live."

What had she been doing for twenty years? Existing in suspended animation?

The cat is upset by the suitcases and boxes and unspoken recriminations. She's hiding. For a moment I fear she's sneaked into the truck, gone off with my daughter on an adventure from which I am forbidden.

She left a mess. Her bathroom is an embarrassment of damp towels, out-of-date cosmetics, hair in the sink, and nearly empty shampoo bottles. Ha! Some grown-up! She can't even pick up after herself. I'll show her. She doesn't want to live with me, doesn't want to be my baby girl anymore, fine. I can be even stinkier than she is.

I bring a box of big black garbage bags upstairs. Eye shadow, face cream, glitter nail polish, and astringent—into the trash. I dump drawers and sweep shelves clear of gels, mousse, body wash, and perfume. I refuse to consider what might be useful, what can be saved. Everything goes. I scrub the tub and sink clean of her. When I am finished, it is as sterile and impersonal as a motel bathroom.

In her bedroom I find mismatched socks under her bed and frayed panties on the closet floor. Desk drawers are filled with school papers, filed by year and subject. I catch myself reading through poems and essays, admiring high scores on tests and reading her name, printed or typed neatly in the upper right-hand corner of each paper. I pack the desk contents into a box. Six months, I think. I will give her six months to collect her belongings, and then I will throw it all away. That is fair. Grown-ups pay for storage.

Her books stymie me. Dr. Seuss, Sweet Valley High, R. L. Stine, Baby-sitters Club, Shakespeare, The Odyssey and The Iliad, romance novels, historical novels, and textbooks. A lifetime of reading; each book beloved. I want to be heartless, to stuff them in paper sacks for the used bookstore. I love books as much as she does. I cram them onto a single book-shelf to deal with later.

I will turn her room into a crafts room. Or create the fancy guest room I've always wanted. But not for her benefit. When grown-up life proves too hard and she comes crawling back, she can stay in the basement or sleep on the couch.

My ruthlessness returns with a vengeance. Dresses, sweaters, leggings, and shoes she hasn't worn since seventh grade are crammed into garbage bags.

Her thoughtlessness appalls me. Did I raise her to be like this? To treat what she owns—what I paid for—as so much trash? No, she left this mess to thumb her nose at me, as payback for treating her like the child she is.

"Fa la la, Mom, I am off to conquer the world, off to bigger and better things. Do be a dear and take care of this piffle."

I am a plague of locusts emptying the closet. Two piles grow to clumsy heights: one for Goodwill, the other trash.

There are more shoes, stuffed animals large and small, knickknacks, felt pennants, posters, hair bands, and pink foam rollers. The job grows larger the longer I am at it. How can one girl collect so much in only twenty years?

It's obvious she doesn't care about me, her father, our home, or anything we've provided. We are the flotsam and jetsam, the detritus of childhood.

I stuff garbage bags until the plastic strains. I haul them down the stairs two bags at a time. Donations to Goodwill go into the trunk of my car; trash goes to the curb. Sweat and sore shoulders fuel my irritation.

My husband has left the house, perhaps to avoid the same fight I wish to avoid.

She left the bed rumpled, the comforter on the floor, the sheets in a tangle. I strip off the comforter, blanket, sheets, mattress pad, and pillows. Once she starts feeding quarters into Laundromat machines, she'll appreciate the years of clean clothes I've provided for free.

I turn the mattress. A large manila envelope is marked "DO NOT THROW AWAY." I open it. More papers. I dump the contents onto the floor. There are old photographs, letters, greeting cards, and notes filled with sappy sentiments, bad puns, and silly nicknames. There are comics clipped from newspapers and book reviews. Every single item had passed from my hand to hers.

"DO NOT THROW AWAY."

Darned kid knows me too well.

I read over a lifetime of inside jokes and shared sentiments. Maybe the pickup wasn't such a bad idea, after all. Maybe it helps her to feel less small in a big world. Maybe, too, the awful summer wasn't for my benefit, but for hers. It's easier to leave when she's convinced she is too angry to stay.

I retrieve garbage bags from the car and the curb. Clothes and shoes go back into the closet. I remake the bed and pile it with stuffed animals. The cat slinks into the room and looks around with suspicious eyes.

Finally she makes a place for herself between a Christmas bear and an Easter bunny.

My husband comes home and calls up the stairs.

"Just straightening up," I tell him. "Can you find some boxes for her stuff?"

He brings up cartons from the basement. "She left a mess," he says.

"I don't mind," I reply.

"She's not coming back," he says. His anger is gone, and now he's sad.

My little baby, my dependent child, isn't coming back. Someday my daughter, the woman, will return for a visit. Mementos of childhood will await her. So will I.

—Jaye W. Manus

Dear Mom

After thirty years, I am finally beginning to appreciate the mother you have been to me. Although Jana is only ten months old, I feel I have learned more about you in the short time since her birth than in all my years of growing up and breaking away.

As I go about my new life of caring for Jana, I constantly wonder, how on earth did you do it? You, who raised not one, not two, but six children. I'm still feeling shock waves from the change and upheaval one child has made in my life, and I know that what I have experienced so far is only a glimpse, the barest hint, of all you went through raising us.

"You learn to sacrifice when you have children," was one of your stock phrases when I was growing up. To you, sacrifice was a necessary virtue, an accepted part of parenthood. But I didn't go for that.

I considered sacrifice not only unnecessary, but unfashionable and downright unappealing as well.

Well, Mom, what can I say? I'm learning.

Lately, I've begun to look on motherhood as an initiation into "real life." I don't think I realized until Jana's birth that the life I'd led previously—relatively free, easy, and affluent—is not the life led by most people—past or present. By becoming a mother, I seem to have acquired automatic membership into a universal club made up of uncertainties and vulnerabilities, limitations and difficulties, and sometimes, unsolvable problems. Of course, the club has its benefits, too.

When Jana wakes from her afternoon nap and, so happy to see me, gives me her radiant full-face smile, I smile back and feel on my own face the smile you used to give me when I woke up in the morning. Or, when Jana does something particularly cute, I'll glance up at Gary, and in the look we exchange I see the one I remember crossing between you and Dad at opposite ends of the dinner table. It was a look full of feelings I never knew until now.

When I hold Jana close to me and look down to see my hand tight across her chest, or when I tuck a blanket around her while she sleeps and touch the skin of her cheek, I see your hands (those hard-working hands with their smooth oval nails, steady and capable and caring) doing the same things. Then

I feel as if some of the love and security you gave to me through those hands is now in mine, as I pass that love on to Jana.

The other day Jana fell asleep against my arm. I must have spent fifteen or twenty minutes staring at her, marveling at the wheat color of her hair, the suppleness of her skin, her perfect tiny red mouth, moving now and then in sleep. What a rush I felt, of love and wonder, of care and luck, and more. I suddenly remembered something I saw on your face last summer, when I was home on a visit shortly after Jana's birth.

We were sitting on the glider swing in the backyard. It was a lovely morning, cool there in the shade, and the air was full of fragrance from your rose garden. I was holding Jana, who seemed to enjoy the gentle movement of the swing.

But I wasn't enjoying anything just then. I'd had a rough night. Jana was six weeks old and had been up every few hours. I, fretful and nervous as only a new mother can be, had been having trouble falling back to sleep between her feedings. I was cranky and tired, and not feeling cheerful about this motherhood business at all.

Sitting on the glider, we talked—or rather, I talked, letting loose my load of anxiety and frustrations on you. And out of the blue, you reached over to touch my hair.

"It's so pretty," you said, an odd expression on your face. "The way the sun is hitting it just now . . . I never noticed you had so many red highlights before."

A little embarrassed, preoccupied with other thoughts and problems, I shrugged off your comment. I don't know what I said, something short and dismissive, no doubt, as I waved away the compliment. But your words affected me. It had been a long time since someone had seen something truly beautiful in me, and I was pleased.

It has taken me this long to realize that the look you gave me that day is the same look I give her almost daily. And it makes me wonder: Is it possible that you still see the miracle in me that I see in Jana? Does the magic continue even when your children are grown and gone and parents themselves? Will I look at Jana in thirty years and still feel the same rush of love for her that I do now?

It almost hurts to think of that kind of love. It's too vulnerable, too fragile. I know well the barriers that spring up between parents and their children over the years, the frictions, the misunderstandings, the daily conflicts and struggles, the inevitable pulling away and final break for independence. I ache to think that someday Jana will grow up and wave away my tentative words of love as I did yours.

What happens to that first, strong rush of love?

Is it lost somewhere along the way, buried beneath the routine practicalities of caring for a growing child? Or is it there all along, unvoiced and unexpressed, until, perhaps, a new child is born and a mother reaches out to touch her daughter's hair?

That, it seems to me, is the real miracle: the way a mother's love is rediscovered, repeated, passed on again and again—as it has been handed down in our lives from you to me, from me to Jana, and from Jana, perhaps, to her own children. It is a gift in itself.

I guess what I've been meaning to say all along is, thanks, Mom.

—Christine Goold

The Power of a Mother's Love

It was an ordinary day. Steam rose from my coffee cup, clasped in my hand as I went through the house, marking the calendar on the refrigerator, tidying, and cleaning. I started to gather up the kids' dirty clothes and then tossed them back onto the floor. Teach them responsibility, I thought, as I wandered aimlessly back through the house, searching for my misplaced cup.

The pealing phone lured me from my chores, a welcome reprieve from dirty underwear, runaway socks, crumbs, and crumpled paper stashed behind and under dusty furniture.

"Hello."

"Mama?"

My oldest daughter's voice struck me, transmitting both joy and pain as I clinched the receiver.

"Honey, how are you?"

"Fine."

The cautious greetings, rigid as a lance piercing the flesh, followed by painful silence exposed the immeasurable void between mother and daughter.

"So," I said, pacing. "Everything okay?"

"Sure."

Again, the exchange of trivialities: it kept me safe from the verbal bashings she'd normally launch, kept alive my smidgen of hope that one day, somehow, we could bridge the distance between us.

Four years earlier, when my daughter turned thirteen, she had moved in with her dad. Had circumstances been different, had the divorce been more civil, I'd have been more receptive and understanding about my daughter's choice. Instead, my children were caught in a destructive barrage of hostility between their father and me. My daughter became a double agent, playing one parent against the other and manipulating both sides to get her way. She had succeeded.

She'd felt my guidelines were too restrictive, my understanding lacking. In her rebellious confusion, she saw me as unfeeling and cruel, the cause of her misery. Although she was legally old enough to choose which parent to reside with, I worried that the excessive freedom that awaited her under her father's sole care was a disaster waiting to happen.

The more I tried to reason with and reach her, the greater her anger and disgust for me became. Then one day I arrived home from work to find my daughter and her father packing away her life. As they drove away, they took my shattered heart with them in those boxes.

I called her every day and refused to let her icy words freeze me out. When I'd drop by to see her, her curses would kick me out the door and down the street like a smashed beer can, and still I'd return. My daughter didn't realize the power of her mother's love.

She began to douse her anguish with alcohol and drugs, while I, helpless to help her, drowned in that knowledge. I sought an attorney but was told there were no legal grounds for removing her from my ex-husband's custody. Feeling defeated and weary, I finally accepted my place as a non-custodial parent; it was the most difficult challenge of my life. I continued to drop by her house and call regularly, to meet with her teachers and principal, and to be as actively involved in her life as I could. She hated me for it.

"Why can't you mind your own business?" she'd scream.

Her bitterness seared my heart like alcohol on an open sore, but I loved her too much and was too concerned for her to acquiesce to her demands to "just leave me alone."

Four years later, I gripped the phone in my clammy palm at the sound of my seventeen-year-old daughter's voice.

"So, what are you up to today?" I asked.

"I just got back from the doctor."

I stopped pacing and palmed my neck as if to hold myself together.

"Doctor?"

"Yes. The pregnancy test was positive."

"Pregnancy test?" I was shocked. "You're pregnant?"

"Yes."

I didn't know how to respond; I dared not rebuke or cry. I forced myself to remain calm, to keep the disappointment out of my voice.

"When are you due?"

I heard her draw a ragged breath. "May fourteenth."

"Are you okay?"

"Just queasy."

"It will pass after a couple of months."

"That's what the nurse said."

She paused, and I sensed a slight opening in her armor. I yearned to embrace her like a small child.

"Are you busy, Mama?"

"Not really."

"I thought I'd drop by."

My heart thumped. "Sure, come on over."

Our meeting was awkward, but the moment I saw her, my arms instinctively enveloped her in a big hug. As I prepared lunch, she told me that her steady boyfriend was the father. Neither of them was working, and they'd made no plans to get married. I sat down next to her at the counter.

"What are your plans?"

"I'm going to have the baby," she said with no hesitation.

I looked at her face, so childlike, and tried to imagine her a mother.

"I'm glad," I said.

Her silent gaze brought tears to my eyes. Then, she smiled at me, for the first time in a very long time.

In the coming weeks, we planned for the baby's arrival. I accompanied her to doctor's appointments, and we shopped for maternity clothes and baby items. Fortunately, her stepfather had continued her health insurance.

I had known from the start that her boyfriend would participate in the pregnancy, and I tried my best to dawdle in the shadows and not interfere. It was difficult, and taxing, to keep silent. He drank too much and loved to party, but so had my daughter. To condemn him would be to condemn her, and I couldn't risk alienating her when she so desperately needed my support. I had to constantly bite my tongue, especially while footing the bill for a child he wasn't contributing one cent to.

Would she marry him? The question haunted me, until finally I asked her.

"No. He's too irresponsible."

Early in the pregnancy, my daughter started bleeding. I took her to the emergency room, but the tests revealed everything was fine. However, as weeks went by, the spotting continued. One morning after my daughter had spent the night with me and was soaking in a hot bath, blood suddenly started gushing from her, staining the water deep crimson. She had just entered her sixth month of pregnancy.

My mother drove my other children to school while I rushed my oldest daughter to the hospital. Panic clutched my heart, and my emotions ricocheted in every direction, until I saw my daughter's frightened face, and the strength of motherly love claimed command.

An ambulance transported her to the university hospital, ninety miles away. I called her boyfriend and sped behind the red flashing lights down the interstate, praying through tears.

For four days, my daughter would bleed and the medical staff would inhibit it. I stayed with her from 7:00 in the morning until 10:00 or 11:00 at night, and lodged a few blocks away, so that her boyfriend could sleep on the couch next to her bed.

On the fifth day, he went out for a while, and my daughter and I enjoyed some private time together. At nightfall, when her boyfriend returned, I didn't mention the stench of alcohol on his breath or his glassy eyes. Later, after he'd passed out on the couch, my daughter suddenly started to bleed profusely, soaking her pajamas and the bed. I frantically buzzed the nurse. As my daughter, draped in bloody towels, was wheeled into the frosty labor room, I sprinted behind, heels clicking on the glossy tile.

Her face looked ashen beneath the intense lights of the labor room, and her eyes shimmered with terror. I clasped her hand, praying silently that her premature baby, my first grandchild, would survive. With every contraction, she'd squeeze my hand. After several hard contractions and no sign of her inebriated boyfriend, she screamed and cried, "Keep him out of here!"

"Are you sure?" I asked.

"Yes," she said, her outraged eyes bloodshot from weeping, her face wincing with pain.

I wiped her sweaty brow and whispered encouraging words into her ear. Her pain intensified, and she arched her back with laborious whimpers.

"Breathe, honey, breathe. Like this," I inhaled deeply, exhaled slowly.

She mimicked me, and hand in hand, head to head, our pants merged into one vital breath.

Suddenly, she howled, "I need something for pain now!"

The nurse stood, ignoring the pleas, and scanned the chart.

"Is she deaf?" my daughter bellowed.

"I'll check with the doctor," the nurse said and scooted out the door.

"I can't take this," my daughter pleaded, as severe pain curled her into a fetal position.

I stormed out, returning with a nurse, shot in hand.

"This will ease it a little," the nurse said. She immediately departed, no smiles, no good-byes.

"What'd you do?" my daughter asked.

"I held a scalpel to her throat," I kidded.

Laughter tumbled from her lips like a soothing waterfall, and then another pain wracked her. Her scream vaulted off the dull beige walls, bringing the nurse back to check her.

"Let's get her to delivery," the nurse announced.

I froze.

"Do you want to come?" the nurse asked me.

Tingles scuttled up my backbone. "Yes."

"Get dressed in these, and hurry."

I quickly donned the blue scrubs and was whisked to the delivery room, where my daughter's legs were already hiked into cold, sterile air. I took her hand in mine, which she continued to crush with each labor pain.

"Push!" the doctor coached.

My exhausted daughter heaved, her grunts punctuating the rawness of the room.

"Harder!"

A grimace scrunched her face as she shoved with all her might, still gripping my hand like a vise.

"I see his head," the doctor said.

My daughter's eyes locked on mine. I nodded, holding her gaze, still holding her hand.

"Here he comes," the doctor said.

My attention switched, and I watched my grandson emerge, as beautiful as his mommy. His tiny body was coated in bloody placenta. He never stirred, not even a quiver.

"I'm sorry," was all the doctor could say. "I'm so sorry."

My daughter and I crumpled into each other's arms, united in unbearable grief. She cuddled her stillborn infant, my dead grandson, and uttered a wrenching good-bye. Her sobs engulfed the cries of healthy babies doors away.

She rode home with her boyfriend. I drove to my home alone, allowing my grief to surface in the solitude. I wailed for my lifeless grandson and wept for my daughter's difficult life. Yet, I felt grateful for the precious, though heartrending, moments I'd shared with my little girl.

One day after the kids had left for school, as I sat in the silence and stillness, sipping coffee and reading my devotional, the phone rang.

"Mama?" I smiled at the sound of my oldest daughter's voice. "I thought I'd stop by."

"Come on over."

I looked out the kitchen window into the cloudless sky. It was going to be a glorious day.

—*Richelle Putnam*

A Mother Knows

Not all women who have children are mothers. You can tell a true mother by the penetrating look in her eye. A mother always knows everything about you. Absolutely everything.

I had such a mother. I could hide nothing from her. When I would walk into the house after pigging out on chocolate cake at the neighbor's, she would glance at me and say, "How many times do I have to tell you not to eat between meals? No dessert for you tonight, young lady."

I looked at her, dumbfounded: How could she see across the street and through the walls of my friend's house, while she was cleaning the bathroom floor?

"How did you know that?" I asked, wiping crumbs from my chin.

"A mother always knows," she said. "I can read your forehead. Hand me the Bon Ami. I see a fingerprint on the doorknob."

When I would race into the house from school, my eyes popping like a choked fish, my mother would simply point to the bathroom door. "How did you know I had to go?" I asked, as I galloped to the toilet with my legs twisted like a pretzel.

My mother would shrug. "I read it on your forehead."

When I got a bit older, her forehead reading became truly remarkable. I could hide absolutely nothing from that woman's penetrating gaze. I would come home from a date, and my mother would scowl ominously.

"Do you know what time it is?" she'd say. "Men don't marry fast girls."

"We were only holding hands, for God's sake," I lied, rubbing my chafed mouth.

"You can't fool me, Lynn Ruth," said my mother. "I can read the whole vulgar story on your forehead. Put some lotion on your face, or you'll look like a raw tomato tomorrow."

Her amazing knowledge of things she could not see sharpened the farther away I was from home. I arrived at college my freshman year, disoriented and lonesome for the very place I had denounced as a suffocating prison a few hours before. As I settled down on the dormitory bed for a good cry, my mother walked in the door.

"You forgot your pillow," she said and handed me

the very one I had used the night before.

I had done my own packing and had shut the door to my room when we left the house to drive to Ann Arbor. My mother was so nearsighted she couldn't see products on the supermarket shelf without her glasses. How could she possibly make out the print on a forehead sixty miles away? Apparently, my mother could also hear the thoughts rattling around in my brain, for she then answered my unspoken question.

"A mother always knows," she said. "I also brought you some brownies and Rosemary Clooney's latest record release."

In my late twenties, I was in a terrible automobile accident. By that time, I had graduated from college and moved out of my mother's house. One night my mother, who always retired promptly at ten with a potboiler novel and a glass of warm milk, decided to watch the eleven o'clock news. She saw a stretcher move across the screen, the body on it flat as a pile of magazines except for two tremendous feet protruding from the sheet. My mother sat up and shook my father awake.

"Get dressed," she said. "We need to get to the hospital. That's Lynn Ruth."

Time did not diminish my mother's amazing intuition. In fact, it became sharper as I grew older. When I married, she read my impending divorce right through my bridal veil. When I began my job search, she knew the results of my interviews before I received the rejection letters. After I'd moved across the country, I sustained serious injuries from a random violent assault. I returned from the hospital with stitches and bruises all over my body. As I staggered into my bedroom, the telephone rang. It was my mother.

"Lynn Ruth," she said. "Tell me what happened." She knew.

Five years later my mother succumbed to cancer. Although I called her every night, I did not go to her until my urge to see her suddenly overwhelmed me. I flew home the next day. She was so small I could barely locate her among the pillows, sheets, and instruments keeping her alive. She held out her wasted arms to embrace me.

"Oh, Lynnie," she whispered. "How did you guess how much I wanted you here?"

"I read it on your forehead," I said through my tears.

"In California?" asked my mother.

I realized then that all women have mothers, but only a few are lucky enough to become daughters in time. I hugged my mother and said, "A daughter always knows."

—*Lynn Ruth Miller*

The Coronation

M y parents shared a room in a Jewish nursing home during their last years together. For five years, my mother fussed over my father, making sure that he put on clean underwear each morning, soaked his dentures every evening, and finished his snack of apple juice and a vanilla wafer every afternoon. They reminded me of the lyrics to the old song that, as a child, I used to play on our wind-up Victrola: "You're the cream in my coffee. . . ." Though normally undemonstrative of their affection for one another, they had always been the cream in each other's coffee, the lace in each other's shoes. He was her one necessity, and when he died, she was lost without him and eighty-seven years old.

The spark that had lit her spirit went out. I tried to think of ways to please her—little surprises: her favorite butter kuchen, fruit jellies, White Shoulders dusting powder. Nothing appealed to her. It put me in mind of when my daughter was a toddler and didn't feel well, and despite my coaxing, she would adamantly refuse to eat, shaking her head and pushing away the bowl. My mother had lost her appetite for life.

I wondered whether there was something she secretly longed for, some material thing that I could give her to lift her spirits. Then it came to me, a wild notion. "Foolishness! Plain foolishness!" my father would have said. But he had never known the secrets of her heart. The more I thought about it, the better I liked my wild, foolish notion. I would buy her a wig, a proper one to replace the outdated hairpiece and braid that she had worn on special occasions for thirty years.

The only special occasions in the old-age home were birthday parties, celebrated by women in faded smocks and pink crepe paper hats and by men in baggy trousers. In all the years she had been at the home, I had never seen her with the hairpiece. In fact, I hadn't seen it at all, not even in her dresser drawer. It was probably on a shelf somewhere in her cardboard closet, a make-do shelter for homeless possessions. Maybe it was under the bed in the same suitcase in which she kept old family photograph albums. It wasn't that she was disorganized or care-less about her things; there was simply barely space for her to turn around in that room. She was an old woman who lived in a shoebox.

For decades, my mother had mourned the loss of her hair, the blond tresses I had never seen. Child-birth followed by double pneumonia had robbed her of it. Hats had become her crowning glory. Never skimpy little hats, but imposing hats with sweeping brims, Cossack hats, velour cloches with dotted veils that swooped under her chin and up over her ears, all fastened in the back with a tortoise-shell hat pin. With her erect bearing and ample form, she was a cross between Ethel Barrymore and Winston Churchill. Birds might have left their droppings on other people's chapeaux, but never on my mother's. When my mother walked down the street, all the little birdies went "Tweet, tweet, tweet."

Her build was extra large, but it suited her grande dame style. In the days before automatic elevators, she would exit with a gracious nod at the elevator operator. "Thank you, kind sir," she would say, as if he were opening the door to her carriage instead of the housewares section of the department store. In a crowded elevator, she always took care not to disturb her hat. But she would gladly have burned all of her hats for the head of hair she had once had.

Before the era of synthetic wigs, stylish wigs were made of the finest human hair and were unafford-able to the average woman. My mother no more considered buying one than she considered buying the Hope diamond. But whenever she saw a wig displayed in the window of an elegant beauty salon, she stood there for a long time, wistfully gazing at it.

I didn't know anything about wigs, but my sister did.

"You pick it," I said. "I don't need to go with you."

I brought it to my mother, all done up in a lovely gift box adorned with a navy-and-white polka-dot organdy bow. Not wanting to disturb the wrapping, I hadn't opened the box. The wig would be as much of a surprise to me as to my mother.

"What's this?" she asked.

"A present."

"I don't need presents."

"It's a surprise." I removed the wrapping and placed the box in her lap. "You get to keep the bow."

She had a tremor in her right hand, and it shook as she felt beneath the layers of tissue. She slowly lifted the wig from the box and held it in her lap, timidly fingering the lustrous silver hair, coiffed and perfectly waved. Though her lips were pursed, her large brown eyes shone. She looked as if she were content to sit there forever, patting and stroking the wig as if it were a toy poodle.

"What do you say we try it on?" I coaxed. Carefully placing the wig on her head, I turned it this way and that until I found the right way to position it. My heart sunk. Though luxurious and finely made, the wig was all wrong for her. There was too much of it. Bouffant-style, it was too lavish for an elderly woman. But, it was bought and paid for; there was no taking it back.

Reaching for the walker, my mother slowly rose from her bedside chair and made her way to the bathroom mirror, the only mirror in her room. Steadying herself against her walker, she stood word-lessly, staring at the stranger in the mirror: the deep-set eyes with creased, hooded lids; the broad face with its web of crisscross lines, sagging beneath the mass of teased, exuberant hair.

Her voice was low and thick. "I look like a gorilla."

I saw the crushing disappointment, the mockery of her mirror reflection. I wanted to reassure her that it wasn't so, that it was her imagination. But it was true. Without the wig, she was an old woman. With it, she was a caricature of herself.

Words tumbled from me. "Don't be silly. It just needs to be trimmed, thinned out, restyled maybe. We'll bring a hairdresser to the home. You'll love it; you'll see."

She said nothing, just turned her back on the mirror and pushed the walker back to her chair.

I thought of the inevitable losses in life and of the heaviest one looming before me, the loss of my mother. I didn't want her to see the tears in my eyes, so I went to the doorway and looked out into the corridor. It was 4:45 P.M., fifteen minutes before dinner. The scene unfolding before me was depressingly familiar.

One by one, they shuffled from their rooms, men and women of every build and size, leaning on their walkers and canes. The women's hair was scraggly, their housedresses drab and shapeless. They stood against the wall with vacant stares. There was an undercurrent of restlessness about them, as if they were waiting not just for their dinner, but also for something else, they didn't know what . . . something, perhaps, to break the oppressive monotony of their lives.

At the head of the line was a short, plump woman. I called her "Mrs. Knish." She was chief busybody on my mother's floor. Her little eyes darted everywhere; nothing escaped her notice. If anything out of the ordinary occurred, she was the first to see it and the first to promptly announce it. She made it her business to know everyone else's business, and she commented on it freely whenever she felt the urge, which was frequent.

At 5:00 P.M., the dinner buzzer rang. I glanced at my mother, expecting to see that she had taken off the wig. But she was still wearing it—partly because it was her way of thanking me for the gesture, and partly, I suspected, because she had a love-hate relationship with the wig. She walked into the corridor holding her head high. Maybe she was pretending she was wearing a hat. My mother had never let herself go, no matter what. In her crisp cotton print dress and round yellow earrings, big as after-dinner mints, she stood out from the others.

All heads turned in her direction. A hush fell over the corridor.

Mrs. Knish broke the silence. "Here comes the queen," she announced in her authoritative, Yiddish-accented voice.

A little flurry of excitement filled the air.

"The queen . . . here comes the queen," they murmured one to the other, like prisoners tapping out a code: Pass it on! Pass it on!

Pressing closer to the wall, they gazed at the thick, shining silver hair swirling coquettishly around my mother's once-handsome face. Although the wig was slightly askew and a loose strand dropped over one ear, she wore it like a crown. The men appraised her out of the corners of their eyes. The women smiled and nodded to themselves as if in reverie. Perhaps they were recalling a time of youth and glamour.

My mother had pulled it off. Not the wig, but the grand entrance. The women followed her into the dining room like royal attendants. Heads slightly cocked, birdlike eyes fastened upon her, they might have been crooning, "Tweet, tweet, tweet."

—*Bluma Schwarz*

Full Circle

I brewed tea in my mother's favorite teapot, poured myself a cup, and gazed at the white cardboard box I had found in her closet. A sheet of paper, taped to the top, was dated a few months before her death. The note read: "For you, my daughter. These items brought joy, meaning, and poignancy to my life."

I took a deep breath, opened the box, and pulled aside a mass of white tissue. On top lay her dainty aqua fountain pen, clasped to a note: "My constant companion since age twenty. With this, I have corresponded with my friends, comforted and advised my children, kept in contact with my parents, and written out my heart's desires on pieces of paper that I burned."

Reverently, I pulled out other items: her cameo ring in a tiny velvet purse, a box with a dozen fragile silver teaspoons nestled in satin slots, a Dutch Bible with gold leaf pages and a silver clasp. On the bottom, in faded shades of blue and red, lay a child's dress. As I lifted it up, a long-forgotten memory took shape in my mind.

My dress. Smocking on the bodice, little puff sleeves, a belt that closed in the back with a button. Made by my Oma, my mother's mother.

I detached an envelope that was pinned to the bodice and pulled out a folded sheet of stationery. I pictured my mother at her desk, the gold-tipped pen wedged between her index and middle fingers, pouring out her heart with these words to me:

This dress was made for the daughter I loved but never completely understood, by the mother I loved, who never completely understood me. You received this gift on your sixth birthday, long ago in that dreadful time when Nazis patrolled the streets and bombs fell at night. Oblivious to the deprivations of war, you wore it to school, played in it, donned it when we visited friends, and would have slept in it if we'd have let you.

When I reflect on your childhood, I see you in that dress, your auburn braids ribboned with strips of the same material. And I see my mother. The two of you playing double solitaire. Shelling peas. Winding yarn, Mother's arms outstretched as she teaches you to make an egg-shaped ball that won't roll. You would laugh. About nothing. Your jokes funny only to each other.

One day during dinner you abandoned your practice of placing a piece of cheese to the side of your plate, a habit you had developed so you could eat it last and savor its taste. This time, you bit off a piece at the beginning of the meal, and you chewed thoughtfully before putting the rest of your favorite food in your mouth.

"You're not saving the cheese," I observed.

"No," you said. "I saved a strawberry when I was with Oma. She told me to eat it right away, because the bomb could fall while we were having our lunch, and it would be a shame if I didn't have my dessert."

You laughed, but to me, it wasn't funny. Bombs fell around us all the time and killed people daily. Irritated, I thought, Mother, how could you frighten our child with this nonsense?

Every June, we visited a cherry orchard near Arnhem. We took the bus to the end of the line, then walked another half mile to the farm. Ladders stood against the trees, and each of us was given a basket. We placed our lunches of bread, cheese, and jam on nearby tables and picked our baskets full of luminous deep-red fruit clusters.

When we sat down to eat our meal, each of you children was allowed to choose twelve cherries for dessert. You spread out your harvests on the table, picking out the largest, darkest fruit.

That year, your cache displayed the biggest jewel in all our findings. You placed it carefully near your plate. I watched with amusement; so did your Oma. She eyed the cherry, then her granddaughter, and I saw a twinkle in her eyes.

Suddenly, she reached her arm across the table, picked up the cherry, and popped it in her mouth.

Anger surging within me, I wanted to scold her, but then I looked at you. You stared with disbelief at your grandmother, now chewing noisily, exaggerated rapture on her face.

A giggle started in your throat. It crescendoed to a laugh. "This is like the strawberry, huh, Oma? And the bomb."

You both laughed so hard, your eyes began to water.

"Yes," Mother said. "Like the bomb."

Then, picking you up, she circled a tree until you saw a huge red cherry just within your reach, and you plucked the ultimate prize of the day.

I understood the lesson she was teaching you, the one she had always practiced: Cherish each day for what it is and find joy amid difficult times. The future is irrelevant.

You have inherited her personality.

I, on the other hand, have always had a squirrel mentality: Save up for the future. Therein lies my security.

What works best? I don't know. Perhaps it is about honoring our own natures.

I love you so much, my daughter. And I am saddened that I did not know how to enter that magic circle you and your grandmother created between you. I've kept this dress as a symbol of that bond. I give it back to you—from her, from me.

I bunched up the dress and buried my face in its folds. I thought about all the times my mother must have held this remnant of our past, wistfully remembering a time, so long ago, when two people who were so important in her life enjoyed a special friendship from which she felt excluded.

With tears in my eyes and an ache in my heart, I asked for her forgiveness. Then, imagining Oma by my side, I invited my mother into the circle.

—*Annemarieke Tazelaar*

Heart Choices

I stand on the seawall of my parents' property in Florida and watch as an elderly woman with a deep tan walks slowly toward a decrepit pier in the distance. Long ribbons of pink and orange sunlight float beneath the darkening sky. The German shepherd walking with her is too busy chasing seagulls to notice me. I watch as the woman bends to the sand, one hand to her lower back. In her left hand she holds a garbage bag filled with the trash she is collecting off the beach. Emotions surge through me as I watch her. The woman is my mother, and we have not spoken to one another in more than five years.

Mom and I have a dark, complicated relationship. During an argument five years earlier, I'd sworn I would never speak to her again. She was angry with me, too, and defiantly cried that that would suit her fine. I'd left her home in a rage, my tires squealing, and both of us had kept to our impassioned promise. But over time, my anger had faded, leaving in its place a feeling of vacancy, homesickness, and incredible loss.

The tone of our relationship had been set when I was around four years old and she told me that she'd never wanted children. She had done it only because, in the late fifties, it was what women did. She'd had no options.

Raised in the hills of Tennessee as the youngest of nine children, Mom had gone barefoot most of her life and had worn dresses made out of burlap bags. When she'd graduated from high school, she tried to leave behind her life of poverty by moving to Atlanta, where she got a job as a secretary. But she could not support herself on the salary.

She married my father when she was thirty, a late age for marriage in that generation. Her new husband came with a two-year-old daughter from a previous marriage and a drinking problem. Mom worked to put him through law school, unwilling to live any longer without some of the niceties of life, and without money or prestige. I was born a few years after my father graduated, and my brother was born seven years later.

The reality was, my mom hadn't really wanted any of it: She did not want a husband and had no interest in raising children. She was a fiercely independent woman born in the wrong era.

Dad started making a lot of money right away in his law practice, and our family acquired material things that my mother had never had before—nice clothes, a big house on the right side of the tracks, and fancy cars. Mom and Dad put on happy faces in public to show that they were a beautiful rich couple with three great kids. But it was all a facade.

Dad's alcoholism and that my sister was a stepchild were the family secrets that festered and boiled. My parents had awful fights in the middle of the night, when they'd scream things at each other that could never be taken back. Dad would storm around the house, so drunk he could barely stand, one time becoming so angry at something my mother said that he ripped all the cabinet doors off their hinges. My sister and I would lie in our bed, holding hands, crying, and praying for the night to end.

During the daytime my mother took out her frustrations on her stepdaughter with a vengeance, eventually driving her off at age sixteen. On the day she left, Mom drove to the house where we knew my sister had fled to and sent me to the front door to tell her to come home. I can still feel the shame of standing on a stranger's doorstep asking to see my own sister.

"She's taking a shower," the other mother said

curtly, and that was the end of it. I went back to the car where my mother sat, morose and sullen, feeling like I had let her down.

We clashed frequently while I was growing up—both of us willful and stubborn—the anger and bitterness fueled by the powerful and confusing feelings that come from living in an alcoholic household. I could not forgive her for the transgressions against my sister or for her clear message to us that she'd never wanted children. I hated my mother for staying with my father, and I despised her for thinking so little of herself.

Once, in a rare moment of contemplation, Mom plaintively told me that she wished she and I could have been friends. I snorted indignantly and walked off, but deep inside I was touched . . . and profoundly sad.

I occasionally got to see the strong, beautiful woman hidden just under my mother's hard surface. When I was five years old, I tried out for cheerleader for the first time, and Mom came down to the dugout where I was waiting for my turn. She leaned her creamy face into mine, dark eyes shining, her lips covered with ruby red lipstick. She smelled like fresh-cut flowers.

"Now remember to yell as loud as you can," she said, smiling at me, a smile I saw precious few times in my life.

When I got before the judges, I remembered my mother's advice and yelled "Ready!" as loud as my five-year-old lungs could bellow. The judges laughed. And I made the squad.

Sometimes my mom would reach over and take my hand as we walked through the mall or the grocery store together, our bodies softly bumping as we strolled. Because I was so much taller than she, it seemed to me that she could have been the child and I, the mother. At those times I felt the old resentments between us fall away, as if the touching of our hands was a special kind of communication that normally eluded us.

When I was nominated for prom queen, Mom fussed for a month over the tiniest details of my dress, the color of the sash at my waist, and how I should wear my hair. After I was crowned queen in the high school cafeteria, she glowed like a 100-watt lightbulb for two weeks. The dress I wore still hangs in her closet.

The real coup came after I graduated from college. Mom had told me literally thousands of times while I was growing up that I would go to college— no ifs, ands, or buts. A college degree was the only assurance a woman had in the world, she often said. It was the only way a woman could avoid the fate she'd been handed, a lifetime of dependence on a man for food, clothing, and shelter. The night of my graduation, she sat across from me at the dinner table and looked at me with deep satisfaction.

"Now, you will never have to depend on a man to support you," she said, nodding at me gravely. "You can have your own life now. You have choices."

In that moment, I understood that I held the ticket to the future she had reached desperately for but never touched. And I felt the familiar mixture of guilt and gratitude wash over me.

By the time I graduated with my master's degree two years later, she had developed a phobia that confined her to the house, so she did not attend the ceremony. She sent my father instead. He was sober for the occasion and waved to me from the stands. Afterward he sent me a note that read simply, "Your mother and I are very proud of you."

When I got married a few years later, Mom stayed in bed for two weeks after the wedding. My brother had long since left, vowing never to see his crazy parents again, a vow that has stuck. Our sister was somewhere out in California, living her own life. Mom was left with our father, and for the first time she had to face a life alone with him, the walking, talking, breathing incarnation of her perceived powerlessness.

A few months ago I decided that the price I was paying for cutting my mother out of my life was too dear. Despite the hurt, despite the pain of the past, she was still my mother. Yes, there had been bad times, but there had been good times, too. It is my choice which of those memories to hold nearest to my heart.

The woman on the beach turns and heads back in my direction. She walks for a long time without looking up, deep in thought, until the dog catches my scent on the air and starts to run and bark frantically. He does not recognize me at first, and then he does, and I pet the wet, shaggy head as he kisses my arms, my legs, my face. When we are done with the greeting, I straighten up and find my mother staring at me. Our eyes lock across the beach, the air between us heavy with humidity. She bends down to retrieve a beer can that has floated to shore during her walk, and my stomach tightens. I have surprised her with the visit, and I am not sure how she will react. I want to smile, but my cheeks feel too heavy for my mouth to lift.

"I try my best to keep this beach clean," she says when she stands up again, looking out over the beach. Her face has aged considerably, but the inherent beauty is still there.

"It looks great," I reply, although this is not what I want to say. What I really want to say is, I'm sorry; can we make another start? Most of all I want to say, Thank you for giving me the chances you never had.

But I say none of this, because suddenly there is a lump as big as an apple in my throat. I blink my eyes hard to keep back the tears that threaten to spill down my face.

Mom moves her gaze from the sand to me.

"I've missed you," she says.

I nod, because my voice is still trapped behind the apple. I notice a blue heron skimming the surface of the water with his belly.

"Here, help me up," she says, holding out her hand so I can pull her onto the seawall.

I take her hand and feel the warm, soft palm in mine. When she is standing beside me, she holds on to my hand for a second longer than she needs to. I tower over her petite frame, which is beginning to hunch with age. She looks up at my face and smiles. It is the smile I remember from my cheerleader try-outs. I see that she has gotten to the same place that I have, and I reach for her hand again. We walk to the house without speaking, our bodies touching, the memory of all that is right and good about our relationship rising up between us.

—*Kelly L. Stone*

Daughter of the Bride

M y mom announced her engagement on my answering machine. It was one of those rare middle-of-the-night phone calls delivering good news, and I missed it. Submerged in a flu-induced New Year's Eve hibernation, my husband and I had turned off the phone ringers that evening and called it a year.

I played the message the next morning, expecting to hear loud greetings from a missed party. Instead, I heard my mom's happily tearful voice announcing the perfect introduction to a new millennium: She was getting married after more than a dozen years of single parenthood, self-taught independence, and dating misadventures.

I immediately phoned home, hating the hundreds of miles between us. This kind of news is best relished in a kitchen counter conversation—a lengthy, looping, mother-daughter discussion held while perched atop the kitchen counters, preferably with ice cream.

When my mom answered the phone, I let out a celebratory shriek and burst into tears. It is an inherited response. Wordless joy, overflowing pride, abundant surprise are all tear-worthy in our emotional shorthand. As my mom described the evening's events that had led to Paul's proposal, memories clicked like so many slides across a silent screen, a progression of shifting relationships that defined personal evolutions.

I remembered my mom curling into bed with me the night that she and my dad announced their separation, anchoring me in love even as she spiraled into unknowable grief.

I remembered telling my mom about my own engagement as we waded in the balmy curve of currents off the Florida Keys, hugging and laughing under an October sun.

I remembered driving my mom to her surprise fiftieth birthday party and watching her walk into a room of women who were family by choice, friends through school, weddings, baby-sitting club, Lake Michigan summers, and unexpected transitions.

I remembered watching my mom speak at her mother's funeral, now a motherless daughter after years of tackling the daily, open-hearted tasks of parenting a parent.

I remembered my mom preparing for her first date with Paul, wary of yet another endless dinner with a stranger who might drone about himself through dessert and then calculate her share of the bill to the penny.

Instead, the dinner had opened a relationship that encompasses past lives, laughter, loss, grown children, compromise, and hope. I listened long-distance to my mom's giddiness and incredulity at meeting such a gentle, thoughtful man—especially now, a beginning after so many endings.

As months went by, I felt like a junior high school confidante, an eager accomplice in the unfurling he-said/she-said girl talk that somehow makes a relationship feel more real. I even fell a little in love myself. How could I not adore the man who so clearly complements my mother?

And now my mom is getting married. This time, she is a bride without the veil, trousseau, or parents to give her away. While she is quite capable of giving herself away, I somehow feel responsible for my mom's heart. For better or for worse, I am a maternal daughter, always taking care, watching out, keeping the peace.

As an unmatronly matron of honor who has a thirty-year history with the bride, I feel I am giving part of the woman I know to Paul. This woman who loves chocolate éclairs, golden retrievers, and late afternoons at the beach with a good book. This woman who is the first to ask what she can do for you, roots for Indiana University basketball, and is always grammatically correct. This woman who sleeps too little, gives too much, and has a gift for hearing what is unsaid.

I think a certain amount of grace is inherent in any transition. For so many years, my mom has been that grace for me, propelling me forward with unconditional love. Now, it is my turn. Next month, when my mom says, "I do," I want her to know that I do, too.

—Molly Hulett

First Moon Rising

When I first heard about the "red party," I was intrigued and excited. Remembering the secrecy and negative feelings that surrounded first menstrual periods in my generation, I felt I owed it to my oldest daughter, Linda, to celebrate this important event. But would she be willing? Or would she be too embarrassed? How would we go about it? Being that we are neither a religious nor a very spiritual family, we have no experience with such rituals and ceremonies.

Linda was only eleven when I mentioned my idea to her, and her first period still seemed somewhat remote. We talked about people she might want to invite; she said she would let me know when the time came if she was interested, and we left it at that. Now and then I would come across something interesting and hide it in a closet—a little statue of a woman, a pair of lacy pajamas, a silk robe in her size.

Then one day Linda came home from school and said, matter-of-factly, "Luckily my friend Sara had a pad with her, because I got my period."

I smiled and congratulated her, while hiding some motherly guilt—"You didn't even make sure to give her a pad to take to school!" We had read books together and talked about it all, but I had neglected this crucial detail.

Well, let me make it up to her. How about that party we'd talked about? She said she would talk to her friends and see what they thought. And what will their mothers think? I wondered. I broached the subject with one of the moms, who immediately responded, "Oh, I think it is a wonderful idea! I've heard about those ceremonies, but I've never been to one."

Once my daughter gave me the green light, I began my research. The woman who first told me about the red party e-mailed me the guidelines for a "maidening" ceremony that her church performed. An old acquaintance who knew of some rituals surrounding the first period said she would be honored to help with the ceremony.

Linda started to get excited once the date was set. "Mom, could we have lots of candles? Or a fire? How about flower garlands? I saw this great way to put my hair up like the Greeks did in olden times. I want to wear something white or red, and it should be long and flowing."

Half of the fun is in planning and dreaming. I wanted my daughter to dream up the most beautiful ceremony; I wanted her to feel as beautiful as a bride, as a goddess; I wanted to celebrate womanhood with her. In striving for equality with men, I had always pushed aside my feminine side. Only when I became a mother did I come to appreciate my femininity. Now, I want my daughters to look in the mirror with pride and to walk down the street like they own the world, confident in their own beauty and worth.

Linda invited two school friends, a younger girl from down the street, and (after some prodding) the elder of her two younger sisters. Two of the moms joined their daughters. Linda also invited some women she had always felt close to and admired—an old family friend, a young woman who had been her science project mentor, and a neighbor for whom she baby-sat.

Meanwhile, I searched the Internet for "menstruation," "menarche," and "red party." I went to the library and bookstores. I talked to other women. Though I didn't find any step-by-step instructions for this rite of passage, I found bits and pieces around which we could design our own ritual: Serve red foods. Wear something red. Include the elements of earth, fire, air, and water. Share stories.

Sing. Tie it all together and see what happens.

I was a bit worried about how a bunch of middle-class women from diverse cultural and religious backgrounds (among others, a devout Christian, a nonpracticing Hindu, a Palestinian, and a Hawaiian) would take it. How would we muddle through? Oh, but we did. And it was a lovely, moving experience for all of us, girls and women alike.

We gathered in the evening as the sun set and the fog rolled in from the ocean. Everyone wore something red, from a bright red-and-gold Indian tunic and pants to a necklace of red beads over a denim dress. The girls set up an altar on a red table-cloth in the middle of our living room floor. They brought in branches from the bay trees surrounding our house and placed the four elements in the four directions: air (east), represented with feathers; fire (south), with a burning candle and smoldering sage; water (west), with a bowl of ocean water and oil; and earth (north), with a bowl of red clay. Between two white candles we placed the daisy garland I'd woven for Linda to wear. We sprinkled red rose petals and other small flowers from the front door to the altar. Each girl held a red candle.

Standing in a circle around the altar, we began with words of welcome and introductions: "I am a daughter of so and so, a mother of so and so, a sister to so and so." Our wise mistress of ceremonies thanked the elements for their presence and talked about what each means in a woman's life. We learned that air represents our thoughts, ideas, and womanly wisdom; fire our passions and sensuality; water our dreams, visions, and intuition; and earth our body and fertility. We held hands and, timidly at first and then loudly from the heart, sang a beautiful American Indian song:

> *River she is flowing, growing,*
> *River she is flowing to the sea.*
> *Carry me my mother,*
> *Your Child I will always be.*
> *Carry me my mother to the sea.*
> *River she is flowing . . .*

Then I passed Linda a box wrapped in red paper. Inside, under many layers of tissue paper, lay a smaller box, crisscrossed by a red velvet ribbon. That box held a small clay statue of the goddess of menstruation.

"Just as Linda had to go through all those layers to get to the little statue," I said, "I would like us to go through all our layers and reach deep inside of us and share our thoughts with her."

As we passed around the statue, we talked about the women we admired, our role models. The girls came up with Amelia Earhart and other women from the past; the women talked about dear friends and an elderly lady from the church who is kind and giving. Of course, we remembered, with admiration and tears, our mothers and grandmothers. The Indian woman told us about her grandmother, who had entered an arranged marriage at age sixteen with a man she didn't love. Another guest spoke about her mother, who had raised seven children. We talked about the struggles and joys of becoming and of being women.

Then it was time for the threshold ceremony. We placed a red velvet ribbon on the floor to separate us into two groups: my daughter, surrounded by her friends, each holding a red flaming candle, on one side, and all the women on the other side. I had asked Linda to bring something that was dear to her and represented her childhood. She chose her oldest stuffed animal, which had a permanent place on her bed. Because I had told her that she would be asked to leave it behind, she had carried it lovingly with her the whole day.

Now she stood, a woman-child, resplendent in a long red dress (my handpainted red wedding dress— I always did fly in the face of convention), her long hair crowned with a garland of flowers, clutching her stuffed animal. In a shaky voice she gave her name in response to the first question, "Who approaches this threshold?" When the next question came, "Are you ready to leave behind your childhood, as you become a maiden?" she whispered, "No!"

"Well," I said, "When you are ready to step over and join our circle, leave your toy behind."

Linda closed her eyes, took a deep breath, and put down her toy. Then she stepped over the red ribbon and fell sobbing into my arms.

"Welcome, maiden, on the path to womanhood," I said.

I touched her with the feathers, saying, "May the air fill your sails and send you soaring."

Circling her head with the candle, I said, "May the fire not scorch you, but make you strong."

Sprinkling water on her, I said, "May the water of life flow freely and gently for you."

Holding red clay over her head, I ended, "May the Earth be a place of joy for you."

Then I offered her a spoonful of honey with the words, "Growing up brings with it the sweetness of life." Sprinkling salt on her tongue, I added, "And also bitterness of life. As you mature I know you will learn to handle both." With a luscious red strawberry came, "May you never hunger," and with a drink of black currant juice, "May you never thirst."

Next, I presented gifts. I placed a heart-shaped necklace around her neck ("May this heart protect you!") and a shell bracelet around her wrist ("May this bracelet embrace you with the love of your family!").

With the flames of their candles, the circle of girls reached over the red ribbon and lit her red candle.

Looking around at the smiling and gently weeping women, I told my daughter, "As you travel on the road to womanhood and you encounter fears and difficulties, remember that you are not alone. Here is your circle of women who will help you and guide you. And remember that I will always be there for you, no matter how heavy your burden."

Then I offered her the stuffed animal with the words, "Even though you are a maiden now, it is always good to know that you have a precious little girl inside you. Keep this as a symbol of your childhood and my love for you."

I had asked everyone to bring a stone and a blessing or a wish. Handing her my stone, on which the words "Follow your heart" were written, I read my blessing, which was inspired and borrowed from different poems I had found:

> "On the Road to Womanhood"
> Be free to be you
> Be strong, yet gentle,
> Be proud, yet loving.
> May your body always be
> A blessing to you,
> A sacred grove of love and pleasure.
> So care for your body
> As you would for a beautiful garden.
> Your womb can now bring forth new life

But remember yours is the power
To open or close the gates of life
In your garden.
Therefore yours is the responsibility
To be a conscious gardener.
Open to the embrace of love
When you find the one
Who is truly deserving.

Each guest presented Linda with a stone and a wish. Some had brought stones with Japanese symbols, others stones from their gardens. My younger daughter had searched the dry streambed for a perfectly smooth stone on which she wrote "Joy, Happiness, Generosity." It was touching to see these two sisters (who usually have more than their share of disagreements) hug and express their love for each other with tears in their eyes. Other stones bestowed blessings of courage, wisdom, health, love, knowledge, strength, and financial independence. Linda wrapped all the stones in a black cloth and tied it with her red velvet ribbon, to keep as a memory and a reminder of qualities she should be striving for. We ended with a Navajo puberty poem:

Watch over me.
Hold your hand before me in protection.
Stand guard for me, speak in defense of me.

As I speak for you, so do ye.
As you speak for me, thus shall I do.

May it be beautiful before me.
May it be beautiful behind me.
May it be beautiful below me.
May it be beautiful above me.
May it be beautiful around me.

Of course, no celebration would be complete without a feast. We filled the glasses with red wine and cranberry juice, and feasted on the wonderful dishes the women had brought: pasta with red peppers, risotto with chunks of red tomatoes, pizza, tomato salad, raspberry mousse cake, strawberries, cherries, and watermelon. And (although it isn't red) a lot of chocolate! It was a magical evening of tears, laughter, and special feelings of connection, sisterhood, and joy in the beauty and strength of women.

—*Ksenija Soster Olmer*

"First Moon Rising" was first published in *Mothering* magazine, November/December 2001.

All names have been changed to protect the privacy of the people in this story.

The Inheritance

I sit on an unfinished windowsill in my unfinished house, listening to the screaming of a drill, the ragged scraping of a saw. Sawdust floats from the upper beams and swirls in a ray of sunlight, then disappears again into shadow. My daughters scamper up and down ladders, unafraid and agile as monkeys flitting across a jungle canopy. Beyond the giant skeleton of boards and beams, I am surrounded by the lush thickness of forest still new in its summer green.

I smoke a cigarette, feel guilty about it, and watch my mother as she picks her way deliberately among the planks, ladders, and scaffolding. She is past her seventieth year now, and my eyes follow her closely, protectively. My daughters are as new with womanhood as the trees are with green, and their steps are sure, fearless. Mama's feet move slowly, heavy with effort, measured with care.

I think about the talk she and I had in the car on the way up to this mountainside, where I soon will live. We don't have a lot of time alone together, Mama and I. With the girls following along in the car behind us and me keeping an eye on them through my rear-view window, watching them bop up and down in their seats to the radio I am certain is set loud enough to blast holes in their eardrums, Mama and I had enjoyed the quiet. Not simply the quiet of my car, but the quiet between us.

She said, "It will be a magnificent house."

I smiled and nodded, checking the rear-view again. They would be furious if they knew how much I still mothered them, in secret.

She said, "It will be something wonderful you can leave to them someday."

I'd already thought of that, several times, and imagined myself leaving little notes for them in desk drawers and other special places, telling them how much I loved them and had always loved them. They could find the tiny treasures I'd left them within the big treasure I would leave to them.

Mama said, "I wish I had something I could leave to you, Camille. Nothing as fancy as a house, but at least something, some small part of me you could always have."

I nodded but did not respond. We both knew she had nothing, no home of her own, no hidden fortune, no material treasures. She sighed again, and I reached over, closed my hand over hers and held her.

The thought emerged slowly in my mind, like the triangular message at the bottom of a Magic 8 Ball. It came up to me through murky waters until it bobbed up and down a few times and then became still.

I said, "You do have something you can leave to me. You do have an inheritance for me."

She turned her head toward me, and I felt the confusion in her gaze. She said, "I don't, Camilletje. I'm so sorry."

The vision took on crisp edges, depth, color, and form. I could see it all. I said, "You leave to me what your mother left to you and her mother left to her. You leave to me the treasure box of stones."

"Stones?" she blinked.

"Stones . . . all silver and shiny, smooth and round. Stones that will glow in the moonlight on even the darkest night."

Mama smiled, patted my leg, and said, "What stones, you silly thing?"

"They have words on them, Mama, and I can read the words, no matter how lost I am, because the stones glow. They say, 'You will be strong because I was strong.' They say, 'You will survive any heartache because I survived all heartaches.' They say, 'You will have courage and wisdom because I had courage and wisdom, and you are my daughter.' Those are the stones, Mama. And that is my inheritance."

She reached for my hand and held it. Her grip was strong; her hand trembled. She whispered, "Yes. Yes. Those stones are for you."

Now, I sit on the unfinished windowsill of my unfinished house, watching my daughters explore and watching my mother run her hands along a beam. She says, "Nice and sturdy."

It occurs to me that, when she dies, I will be the loneliest person in the world. I feel a stinging in my nose, and my eyes fill with tears. I blink them away and continue watching Mama. Her head is up, her gaze intense. My daughters are calling, "Grandma! Come look at this!" Then, they stand together at the edge of the house where no walls have yet been built, and they point beyond the precipice to the rising, flowing mountain ridges, all dusky and blue.

I remember Mama when she was young, when I was young. There were "nice" mamas in my neighborhood and "mean" mamas. There were more than a few "scary" mamas. Mine, I recall with fresh pride, had always been the "pretty" mama—her dark hair and knowing brown eyes, her wicked smile and the way she shamelessly let her hips swing from side to side when she walked. There was not a child who didn't adore her, not a man who didn't notice her, and not a woman who didn't envy her.

My mama, from whom anger flared and laughter bubbled with equal force. I worshipped her, hated her, confided in her, lied to her. My mama, whose childhood had been ripped from her in a concentration camp. My mama, who had survived two marriages to husbands not man enough for her and who had reared five children nearly single-handedly. Seeing her now, standing with my daughters, I let the knowledge of her age sink into my heart.

I think, What will I do when you die? Who will I talk to? Who will love me like you always have? I'll be alone, Mama. I'll be alone.

I see, in my mind, a treasure box, the lid standing open, shiny silver stones stacked inside it. I am her daughter. I'll be strong, because she was always strong. I'll survive any heartache, because she survived all heartaches. I'll have courage and wisdom, because she had courage and taught me to be wise. And, no matter how dark it gets, if I am patient and wait for the rising moon, the stones will show me where to point my feet on the most tangled path.

I realize I am crying, and suddenly, she is standing there in front of me. My girls have wandered off, and Mama and I are alone. She says nothing. I lean forward and press my face against her. She holds me, strokes my hair, and says, "Mothers never leave their daughters. Don't you know that? They are woven together, heart to heart, soul to soul.

Even death cannot break that bond. When I am gone, remember the stones, and I will always be close to you."

I hold her fiercely and murmur, "I'll remember, Mama. I'll always remember."

—Camille Moffat

Lessons from a Four-Year-Old

"Okay, time out," I tell Katie, fed up with the little power struggle we're having over bedtime.

She protests, but resigns herself to a corner for the four minutes. Forgetting it's dark in there, I pull the door almost closed. She cries and says she's scared.

"Be scared," I suggest, obviously in need of a time-out myself.

The four minutes are tough on me. Katie hardly ever needs discipline, and it's foreign territory. When it's over, we hug and talk. Since I yelled at her, we decide maybe I need a time-out, too. Her eyes light up. A little order is restored to her kid universe.

"Four minutes!" she announces, with great relish. I congratulate myself on the creative parenting, while she pauses at the door. Her eyes are wet. "I won't close it," she says. "I don't want you to be scared."

I think I'll spend my time in the corner crying, too.

Giving birth to Katie was like taking on a personal trainer—for life. I supply the breastmilk, training pants, and Barbie dolls. She provides a moment-by-moment reminder of what's important.

The hair salon is always noisy, but Katie silences it on her first visit.

"I love you, Gloria!" she exclaims, settling into her chair for a trim.

She's known her only ten minutes, but in that time Gloria has washed her hair without getting soap in her eyes, massaged her scalp, and given her a sucker to help her sit still. What's not to love? The words hang in the air, though. No one knows how to react. We're not used to saying "I love you" to one another, not to people we barely know, not at ten o'clock in the morning. At least one of us is wondering what kind of world it would be if we were.

"Hi, sweetheart!" a bank teller greets Katie, handing her another sucker.

"Hi, cutie!" Katie fires back.

From the look on the woman's face, it's been a while since anyone has called her "cutie." My smile confirms it: You heard her right. "What the heck?" she tells Kate, and gives her stickers, too.

Katie's exuberance is occasionally interrupted by

a little meltdown when she's tired. She is a kid, after all, and the world ends when things go wrong. My husband is uncomfortable when she cries. He swoops down and tries to solve the problem, but in the process creates a new one: Even though the problem may be fixed, she needs to feel badly and cry a while longer, but she knows he disapproves.

I almost love it when she cries. She sits on my lap, and we chat. "What happened?" I ask. She tells me. "That sucks," I agree. "That really sucks." We wax poetic on how cleansing a good cry can be. Maybe she feels better or maybe she gets bored, but the tears subside.

Now that she's ready, Katie and her dad, who is still anxious to help, tackle the problem together.

"Hearts are popping out of me!" she tells him.

"Huh?"

"Like in the cartoons," she explains.

Before Katie came along, grocery shopping was a painfully boring chore. Now I make sure we never get through our list, so that we have a reason to come back in a day or two. She wants me to admire her reflection in the mirror above the produce, negotiates for still another sample, reminds me that girls live for chocolate and wants reassurance there's plenty at home.

By the time we reach the checkout, I ask her, as I have before, "Do you ever stop talking?"

"Never!" she says, proudly.

"Yackety-shmackety!" I tease her with a nick-name one of my girlfriends assigned her because of her chattiness.

"Yackety-yack, don't talk back!" she whispers in a silly voice.

I tickle her. She giggles.

The line is moving slowly, and we're going to be there a while. Not a problem.

"Yackety-yack, don't talk back!" Katie whispers in my ear again and waits to be tickled.

The giggles build to a crescendo, and soon every-one around us is infected. We can't stop laughing. I try to remember what was boring about grocery shop-ping. You can have your trips to the Bahamas and weekends in New York City. Just send me back to the store with my preschooler for more milk and bread.

When I was a teenager, my little sister got ham-sters and continuously pestered our dad to watch them play. "Kids have the secret to life," he told my mom and me. "I watch the hamsters, but I'm thinking of all the other things I should be doing. To a kid, that hamster is the only thing in the world."

I was lucky, growing up, to have so many of the adults in my life tell me that their biggest regret was not appreciating their kids more when they were little. Determined to keep that from happening, I did everything right. I nursed Katie around the clock for two years, designed my work so she's almost always in tow, and when she asks me to play I almost always say yes.

But time is a formidable opponent, as I learn one summer evening when the local newspaper arrives. School officials are pushing for all-day kindergarten, and when Katie is five she'll likely be in it. There is a hole inside where my stomach used to be. I feel as if a half year of her life has been ripped away from me. Next fall, kindergarten. Then, it's off to college. Or so it will seem. I can't even breathe, I'm crying so hard—but Katie knows what to do.

She crawls up on my lap, hugs me, and doesn't let go.

—*Maureen Anderson*

To Love a Stranger

Aparent since she was fifteen, my seventy-
six-year-old mother used to long for the day
when she could just sit and do nothing. No more
taking care of the children. No more worrying about
whether there was enough money to pay the bills. No
more responsibilities.

She got her wish. Every day now, she sits in a
nursing home, tapping her fingers on her chair in a
syncopated rhythm that reminds me of bebop,
talking to herself about her father, who died when
she was eight.

"Mildred . . . Mildred," I say.

She looks up at me, her eyes brighten, and her
smile reveals snaggles like those of a five-year-old.
"Come here, baby doll," she says.

I rush over to her, pull close a chair, and sit down.

"Hey, Mildred, how are you?" I don't call her

Mommy anymore. She doesn't answer to Mommy.

My mother was diagnosed with Alzheimer's in 1984, right after I graduated from college. While in school, I saw signs that something was wrong. Often, when I would call home, she would be upset because she'd lost her money. "Mommy never loses her money," I'd think.

I fought the disease. Through changes in doctors, diet, and medicine, and through the addition of Chinese herbs, my mother's health improved. She lost seventy-five pounds and regained her ability to converse with other people. Yet, despite profound physical improvement, the Alzheimer's continued to unravel her mind over the next six years.

I lived with my mother from 1984 to 1990, as the illness slowly took its toll. It was appalling to watch her change right in front of me. She didn't just forget things. She became a different person—one whom I did not recognize. When my boyfriend would watch television, she'd walk in circles around his chair, muttering under her breath and scowling. She kept a hammer hidden in her room and wielded it at the slightest provocation. If she got out of the house, she'd refuse to come back in. Instead, she would run down the street, calling for the police to help her. She'd come to believe that she was a police officer— a conviction touched off by a letter inviting her to take the civil service test. Only another police officer could convince her to come into the house.

This is not my mother, I would tell myself. My mother had no interest in men; this person called men over to her window. My mother never cried, yet this woman broke into tears at the slightest thing. My mother always appeared polite and good-natured. This woman was quick-tempered and slightly paranoid. She moved magazines, silverware, dishes, and clothing around the house. When I asked about the objects, she'd become angry and yell at me for thinking she had done something wrong. She told me that other people, not she, had moved these things.

"Come here," she'd say forcefully, grabbing my hand and pulling me into her room. "Listen. Do you hear them? They took it."

To learn more about the disease, my sister and I attended groups for families of Alzheimer's patients. We learned not to blame my mother for things she said or did. The Alzheimer's was talking, not her.

As the disease progressed, my mother grew frightened. She'd say, "What's happening to me? Why can't I remember?"

Before Alzheimer's, my mother never admitted fear or sadness to me. Now, she became strangely free with her emotions, crying when frightened, expressing anger when furious, and laughing when exhilarated. As I released my perceptions of who my mother was supposed to be, we both became calmer.

I used everything I could to stay connected to her as she lost the ability to engage in the hallmarks of linear life. My mother had always loved dancing. When I came home from work, I'd turn on Tina Turner or Janet Jackson, and we would dance and dance. I'd play her favorite songs on the piano, and she'd place her hand on top of the old upright and sing each note and every word perfectly.

As my mother's illness progressed, I saw that I could not provide the care she needed, so I decided to put her in a nursing home. Now that she's away, I dread the day when she will no longer know me. Sometimes she seems lost to me. But then something happens, such as my wedding. Even though she expressed no interest, I needed her there. On my wedding day, she marched in with my father, step-mother, aunts, uncles, and cousins. She sat behind me, occasionally murmuring in time to the minister's speech as he poured libations. When it came time for me to stand, she looked at me and sang out proudly, "That's my gal." I turned to her. "Yes, Mom, it's me."

When I visit her in the nursing home, we don't carry on typical conversations. Rather, I talk about my day and act out Anansi tales. Or I massage her arms, shoulders, and hands. She grabs my arm and cradles it, talking all the while about how she loves babies. And when I feel like a baby myself, wishing I could just tell all my troubles to my mother and know everything will be all right, she holds my hand tight or pats my head, and I'm comforted.

When I tell people, their faces drop. "You poor thing," they say. Perhaps they tell me about loved ones who became unrecognizable as their brains degenerated, ravaged by Alzheimer's.

Those who pity me, however, do not know the whole story. While I hate the disease, I have learned to accept and be nurtured by this new Mildred, who still maintains the essence of my mother. My knowledge of my mother is in my very skin, as is her knowledge of me. Not even Alzheimer's can take that away.

—*Sande Smith*

"To Love a Stranger" was originally published as "A Mother-Daughter Bond Survives Alzheimer's" in *Health Quest: The Publication of Black Wellness*, October 31, 1996.

What I Wanted to Tell Her

"So tell me: What can I expect now that I know I'm having a girl?" my niece asked me as she gently caressed her expanding belly. "I mean, I know I'll be losing some sleep and cleaning lots of poopie. But what is it like to have a daughter?"

Remembering back to the birth of my daughter, I wanted to tell my niece how she would forget the discomfort of pregnancy and the pain of childbirth but would always remember the first time she'd held her newborn daughter and smelled her sweet aroma. I wanted to tell her that the exhaustion of sleepless nights would disappear the moment her daughter looked into her eyes and smiled. And how her heart would melt when she realized that, even before her daughter could understand her words, she understood her love.

I wanted to tell my niece how she would soon look at her own mother differently. How she would memorize her new daughter's every bump, every curve, every inch of skin, and would immediately want to call her mom to apologize for insisting on getting that little tattoo on her hip . . . the one that "no one can see." She would finally understand what her mom meant when she replied, "I'll know it's there." I wanted to tell her how her mother would become wiser each day, because she knew what to do for diaper rashes, grass stains, and bellyaches. I wanted to tell her how much more she would love her mother for loving her. And want to thank her for it.

I wanted to tell her how "sacrifice" would no longer have a negative connotation and would become an honor, a privilege, and a way of life. I wanted to tell her how her heart would break every time her daughter's did. I wanted to explain how she would want to rid the world of hurt, hate, prejudice, and bias—not just for her little girl's sake, but for the sake of every little girl.

I wanted to warn her that her daughter would sometimes embarrass and frustrate, even anger, her. How her delicate flower might develop a knack for passing gas at church or for picking her nose during the Christmas pageant. How she wouldn't know whether to laugh or cry when the pastor's mother said, "Don't worry. All my kids were gassy nose-pickers too, and they turned out just fine!"

I wanted to tell her of the bond she will have with

every other woman of a daughter and of how she would see her daughter in every little girl's eyes. I wanted to explain why she would soon understand what the term *mamma bear* means. And how she would finally understand why her ninety-year-old grandma still calls her sixty-year-old daughter her "little girl."

I wanted to explain how horrified she would be when her little girl wandered away from her at the grocery store. How her heart would pound and her stomach would clench as she ran frantically around the store, searching for familiar pigtails and calling out her daughter's name. How her jubilant tears would fall when her daughter came running to her, saying, "I was just getting the pudding for you." And how she would hug her little one tightly and silently thank God that her beloved child was safe in her arms.

I wanted to tell my niece that she would see her husband through new eyes. She would begin to notice the little things, like how he holds his breath every time their little girl is up at bat. And how, no matter how many times their little slugger might strike out, he always assures her that she's bound to hit a homer sometime and then practices with her in the backyard again and again. I wanted to explain to my niece how much more she would love a man who plays hopscotch with his daughter and braids her hair. And how the love between husband and wife would grow as they watched their daughter grow.

I wanted to tell her how frustrating it would be to see her daughter make mistakes, especially the same ones she'd made. I wanted to reassure her that her daughter would learn from them, just like she had. And I wanted to tell her how hard it would be to let go, to allow her daughter to become her own person, to follow her own dreams.

I wanted to tell her that no matter what might happen, her daughter will always be her daughter, and she will always be her mother. Yes, her daughter will change, and so will their relationship. She will go from being her little girl's best friend to her teenage daughter's nemesis, to her college daughter's relief counselor, to her adult daughter's wise counsel, and finally, back to her best friend again. She would hear "I hate you" along with "I love you"—but will always be loved. And their love for one another would be resilient, permanent, powerful, and unconditional.

A chuckle escapes my lips and tears well in my eyes at the thought of all the magnificent things she will experience as the mother of a girl. But when I look into my niece's puzzled face as she's wondering what's come over me and waiting for me to share what it's like to have a daughter, I simply say, "It's wonderful. Absolutely wonderful."

—Sylvia E. Sheets McDonald

The Bike Trip

During the summer of 1956, my mother nearly gave her friends, her fiancé, and her boss heart attacks. She decided to quit her job as a schoolteacher, leave her friends, and cancel her wedding plans so that she could ride a three-speed Schwinn across the country. She was bored and poor and not in the mood to get married and settle down. No more talk about wedding gowns, no more lesson plans, and no more midnight kisses with her fiancé, Charley the Chest, who wanted to own a gas station and pave America. She was going to see the country, get to California and surf—or at least find the surfers. She convinced an old friend from Girl Scouts to come along. They trained by riding around the streets of Brooklyn, New York, exactly twice. Life was an adventure. What more could she need than to follow the sun to the Pacific?

She packed a bathing suit, a camping shirt, Bermuda shorts, saddle shoes, a cocktail dress, pearls, stiletto heels, lipstick, and a Bible. She wanted to leave room for treasures she might find—cowboy hats from the cowboys she skinny-dipped with; keys to the cities she rode through; tire-patch kits; a bell for her bike; a camera; a journal; cigarettes; etchings; and autographs from mayors, store owners, family friends, and strangers who'd watch her pedal through town. She was an alien creature, this girl of the fifties, thumbing her nose at life's expectations of her, and she imagined the country opening wide to get a taste of her. She was one who was unafraid.

Along the way, Mom and her friend would go to the preachers in the small towns they rode through and ask where they might sleep and eat that night. If the ministers' families didn't have room in their homes, they would let the girls camp on their lawn or find another place for them to stay. These kind strangers always provided a free meal and filled their bicycle bags with leftovers, too.

Out West, Mom slept under the wide-open skies and practiced cowboy songs. Good thing, too, because once she was asked to sing with the house band before a crowd at a Colorado Springs hoedown. I've seen the picture in her scrapbook of her onstage in front of the microphone with a big giggling smile, wearing her patched-up shorts and two-toned shoes. One of the

men in the audience came up and gave her his cowboy hat to "shield her from that hot western sun." As
she finished and walked away from the stage, an elderly woman handed her a folded-up dollar "for a cold
ice tea or something else along the way."

When she finally arrived in California, she went
on a blind date on a whim and a dare, fell in love,
and married a man who looked great in tan pants
and who later became my father. For reasons
unknown, he entered the ministry soon after they
married. Maybe it was his hallelujah for finally
meeting the woman bicyclist of his dreams, or maybe
he was just scared as hell and needed help from the
Big Guy once Mom got ahold of him. No one but the
two of them will ever know—least of all me.

Looking at their very different lives confused me
as a kid. In one corner was Dad, the conservative
Episcopalian minister who quietly grew gardens in
our backyard; in the other was Mom, inviting beach
hippies home after reincarnation meetings at the
Edgar Cayce Institute to climb trees that swung in
the wind. Mom and Dad got along as yin and yang,
Mutt and Jeff, Yoko and John, and I wanted part of
that magic. Hanging out underneath the porch, a
rather chubby girl with an out-of-style pixie haircut,
I'd contemplate the possibilities of being like one of
them. But I was hardly raring to lead a congregation
in choral selections or to be in charge of the altar

guild with all the polishing that task entailed. Nor was I ready to swing or climb, or to learn through regression therapy that I had been an Egyptian cat in one of my past lives.

Mom told and retold her bicycle story to scores of church folks, neighbors, and people in line at the grocery store, and one day I really began listening to her and imagining myself on that trip, smiling hard at the cameras that always seemed to follow her and swimming bare-naked with hooting cowboys. I realized that my mother was a celebrity, and here I was living in the shadow of adventure, of overwhelming excitement. Thoughts of following in my mother's pedal-steps festered and stewed inside my head as I grew up. They kept me company as I pressed my feet into saddle oxfords in junior high school, plastered my winged Farrah Fawcett hair up and out with Aquanet in high school, and tried every major available to me in college.

To some I seemed directionless, a ne'er-do-well, a girl who picked and nibbled at her life instead of devouring it. But I knew my fate was sealed, I knew the direction I had to go, and, in 1996, after many jobs, many ruined relationships, many wrong turns past the exit ramps of life, I met and married Brian, who thought I wasn't a bit crazy for wanting to ride my bike across the country. He didn't care if we maxed out our credit cards or if we didn't have jobs when we returned from the trip. He went along with it, and we rode.

Mom was at home in Virginia Beach when Brian and I followed her route forty years later. And it drove her crazy, because she wanted to be with us. When we talked each night on the phone, she wanted to know every crack in the road, every meal we'd eaten, every skinny-dipping hole we'd found. It got to be somewhat of a nightmare as her questions, concerns, and suggestions focused on why we were taking the easy way out. My mother camped in farmers' backyards; we stayed in Motel 6s. She rode a fifty-pound three-speed; we rode twenty-four-speeds with shocks. She ate rib-eye steaks and drank Manhattans; we did Taco Bell and bought six packs. She wore saddle shoes and Bermuda shorts; we looked like space aliens in our polypropylene.

I'm not proud to admit it in the age of Power Bars, good HDL/bad LDL, and marathon treks up the Himalayas, but we were the loser yuppies to her female Kerouac. She was a yodeling cowgirl who lived out of her saddlebags and would slip into stiletto heels to go out on the town at the end of the day. I was happy just to recoup in a hotel room, flipping the remote control and drinking a light beer.

"Why aren't you camping?" she'd ask.

"Because we like beds," I'd say.

"Are people letting you sleep in their barns?"

"We don't want to sleep in barns."

"Why are you wearing all that fancy gear? You look like scuba divers. I didn't need all that crap."

"It's the way of the world now, Ma," I'd answer from some motel room. "I'm not as tough as you were."

"Like hell you aren't." She'd cackle, and I'd see her sitting in the backyard, holding a Marlboro between her fingers, letting the smoke rise to the pines. "You're just like me."

A scary thought. Was I becoming her by riding this bike or just taking her adventure as a blueprint for my own? Would I become a Marlboro-smoking, wood-chopping wonder who thumbed her nose at society but opened her eyes to the world? I'd smile, feeling the tough armor of her pride in me, then wonder, is this something to aspire to or run away from?

Then she'd add, "Twenty-four speeds? I only had three."

"I'm not riding for three months, like you did. Just fifty-five days."

"Well, I stopped and smelled the flowers. Didn't rush around." Her words were quick and filled with pepper.

"I have a job to get back to," I parried.

"Why didn't you quit?" A jab. "I did." An uppercut.

"I need the money."

"So get a job in the Grand Canyon, like I did. Be a chambermaid and earn some tips."

We were throwing the punches of mother at daughter and daughter right back at mother, yet the love behind our lively thrusts managed to soak into me each night over the phone.

"I could come along for some of the way," she'd always say at the end of the conversation. "Rent a Winnebago and find you out on the road."

"No," I'd say, and she'd stay quiet for uncomfortable moments. I'd listen to her breath on the phone and see her eyes, steely, staring out the window. It would be so easy to say Yes, come on out, find me, lead me to the destination, ease it all for me, Mom— but I didn't. This was something I wanted to do for myself.

"I'm just so proud of you," she finally said one night, and I remember holding the phone tightly between my hands. She repeated it, and it was as though all her other words vaporized, all the pressure disappeared. I wanted to see her face, hold it gently in my hands.

The days seemed to shorten as we went west, and I wanted to make time stand still for long moments, to soak in the movement of Brian and me on bicycles going forward. To finish the journey meant going back, and this sense of riding forward was more tranquil. But the day came, and as we stopped at a lookout above the mountains of Oakland, California, I closed my eyes and held the moment. It had a taste of cornfields, of sea salt, of hot sun on asphalt, of Colorado snow. I swallowed it whole as we rode down to the ocean, where my mother, father, brother, and friends had formed a welcoming party.

I guess you never get over being bested by your mother. But when I hit that Pacific beach with Mom trailing me, as she loves to do, with her old 110 camera minus a battery, I felt a dynasty falling. It was no longer her life and my life, but a shared story-telling of our lives together. Of something done well, or, in my case, simply done. The insistent voices of my childhood, this dream of discovering something found through her, were now all golden.

—Peggy Newland Goetz

A Mother's Arms

I drove to the hospital, the rain misting my windshield, the wiper blades squeaking across the glass, hoping that I'd find a parking space close by. I'd left my umbrella, and I didn't want the documents to get wet.

I prayed a silent "thank you" as a car left a spot near the entrance, and I sprinted to the revolving doors, clutching the papers that represented the hopes and dreams of my clients, Jim and Joelle Markenson.

I ducked inside and inhaled the hospital scent, entered the elevator, and pushed the button for the third floor: maternity. It had been five years since my daughter had been born here. As I walked down the hall, memories flooded me: the long hard labor, hours of pain, followed finally with exhilarating joy at the announcement, "It's a girl!" Later, when they took her to the nursery to monitor her, I tried not to worry. What if she stopped breathing? What if she needed me? Then, relief and profound love filled my heart when the nurse brought my infant daughter to me and I held her close.

I walked past the nursery. No babies there tonight. They were all safe in their mother's arms, in the rooms behind closed doors. The hallway seemed strangely quiet . . . and long. At the end of the hall, I finally came to the room number I'd scrawled on the yellow legal pad: 347. I took a deep breath and knocked. "Come in," someone called.

There on the bed sat Vicky, a pretty natural blond, dressed in a nightshirt, looking even younger than her twenty years, cradling a newborn with jet-black hair. She introduced her daughter as Felicia.

"She's beautiful," I whispered. I envisioned Jim and Joelle arriving tomorrow, seeing her for the first time, their hearts skipping a beat.

"So, do you have papers for me to sign?" she asked, stroking the infant's hair.

"No," I replied, smiling. "We have to wait for the social worker to return with the hospital forms from the nurse. We need the medical information about the birth."

She nodded. "I think they're looking for the nurse right now." She paused. "Do you want to hold her?" she offered, extending her arms.

"Sure," I replied eagerly. As I sat down, I swallowed hard and fought back tears. The baby looked perfect. "So, how are you feeling?" I asked Vicky.

"Good," she replied. "A little tired."

I said, "You look good. And so does she." I looked at Vicky with wonder, admiring her resolve. I wanted to say so many things—to reassure her, congratulate her, commend her. But I was Jim and Joelle's attorney, so I had to guard my words. I was there to pick up the forms from the social worker, review a few documents, and make sure Vicky knew the time of the hearing.

"Did you talk to Jim and Joelle?" she asked.

"Yes," I replied. "They're on their way into town right now."

"That's good," she said and looked away.

I gazed at the baby again. Jim and Joelle's dream was coming true before my eyes. They'd told me that the nursery was ready. I caught myself holding my breath. In three days, we would be at the courthouse, and this courageous young mother would hold a pen in her hand and sign her consent to have the Markensons adopt her child. Would she be able to do it?

The social worker came back in, interrupting an awkward lull in our conversation. "Okay, Vicky, are you ready to sign this?" she asked.

"This isn't the consent, is it?"

"No," replied the social worker. "That you will have to sign in court. This is the preliminary paperwork that tells about the birth and confirms that you've talked to me about your decision. Remember?"

"Oh, yeah." She took the pen.

She signed. I stepped forward, feeling a little bolder now that the social worker was there to represent Vicky. I handed the baby to Vicky. She cuddled her close to her chest.

"Vicky, here are the papers you will sign in court," I said. "The hearing is on Tuesday afternoon at two o'clock. Do you have someone to go with you?"

"Yes, my friend Maya will take me."

"Good." I tried to smile a reassuring smile. "I'll see you in the lobby."

She didn't reply, but instead looked at me with a frown, and then looked longingly at her baby girl. "I . . ." she started, then stopped.

I touched her shoulder gently and smiled. "When you get to the court, we will meet in an office with the magistrate. We will sit across the desk from her, and she will ask you a few questions. It is not at all like a big courtroom. And Maya can be there right beside you."

"What about Felicia?" she asked, stroking her face.

"She will stay here in the nursery until you get back. And then . . ."

She stopped me. "Yeah, I know the rest." She

took a deep breath, exhaled slowly, and then nearly smiled. "Jim and Joelle will be wonderful parents. I wouldn't want anyone else to raise her. They're the only ones." Her eyes shone with determination now. "I'll be there."

I smiled again, but my throat was tight. I stood in awe at the strength and trust of this young woman. She touched the baby's cheek tenderly. The baby's eyes opened for a moment and fixed on Vicky's face. Someday this child would understand her first mother's love.

I realized I was staring, intruding into a sacred space. "I'd better go. See you Tuesday, okay?" I gently patted the baby's soft hair and left.

The long corridor went by in a blur as I thought of all the legal details to cover. When I finally got to the door, I was relieved to see that the rain had stopped. The sun was setting in a stream of pinky orange.

A smile crept across my face as I realized that on the other side of the world the sun would be rising now, painting the sky, and perhaps bringing a smile to another baby girl—the toddler who would join my own family so very soon. I had her picture in my wallet. I knew only that she was fifteen months old, already walking, and waiting in an orphanage in Lishui, China, for her forever mama and forever baba.

"Li Hang," I whispered. "Soon, very soon, we'll see you."

I tried to picture a Chinese mother on a chilly February morning, wrapping her newborn daughter in the warmest coat she could find. Did she talk gently to her? Did she hold back tears so the baby wouldn't hear her cry? How did they arrive at the orphanage hours before dawn? They were so careful, so that no one would see her lay the child on the steps. Did she hide behind a tree and watch? How could she not?

I could almost see a young caretaker opening the door, sticking out her head to see if the cry was a bird . . . or a baby. I imagined the look of compassion as she ran to pick up the bundle and bring her inside. "*May yo gwan she,*" she might have cooed: It will be all right.

We would leave for China in just two weeks. In the meantime, I had to focus on the Markensons' adoption.

The next few days were filled with phone calls. Jim and Joelle tried hard to hold back their excite-ment and delight at the prospect of bringing home a baby daughter. But as soon as they saw her, they fell in love. They called her Gracie.

Each day, sometimes every hour, seemed to bring another roadblock. The process was especially com-plicated because the adopting parents lived in a dif-ferent state. That meant two sets of laws, two different bureaucracies. Each roadblock would loom

like a mountain on the horizon. The Markensons
would pray and wait . . . and pray. They visited with
the baby in the hospital, while I made countless
phone calls, filled out form after form, and double-
checked every detail. We found out that it would
take about thirty-six hours longer than usual to get
the baby released from the hospital. More breath-
holding. More praying.

Then the day arrived. I met briefly with the pro-
bate court magistrate; then Vicky walked in with her
friend Maya. We all sat in comfortable chairs. The
magistrate sat on the other side of a large wooden
desk. Vicky was dressed neatly, her long blond hair
shining. We each raised our hands to be sworn in.
Vicky politely responded to each question from the
magistrate. "Yes," she repeated, as the magistrate
asked her if she was sure she wanted to give up her
right to parent the child. Her voice did not waiver.
Her eyes were intent. She explained how she had
known the adopting couple for years. She told of how
she had personally chosen them to be the baby's parents. She knew she could not raise the child, at least
not in the way she wanted the child to grow up. The
magistrate nodded with compassion and leaned back
in her chair.

I held my breath as the magistrate handed her
the consent form. "This is it, isn't it?" Vicky asked.
She bit her lower lip.

"Yes," the magistrate replied. "When you sign this, you are releasing your child for adoption."

Vicky leaned over the desk, picked up the pen, and carefully signed her name with graceful looping letters. Maya put her hand on Vicky's shoulder to say, "It will be all right."

Then it came. Tears trickled down Vicky's cheeks. Her voice cracking, she managed, "I can't be here anymore." Maya put her arm around Vicky and walked her quickly to the door. I fought back my own tears. I tried to collect my thoughts while I gathered my papers. I left the room and let my tears flow as I walked down the hall, to the elevator, and out to the street, and then I wiped them away. I had to concentrate.

I reached for my cell phone and dialed the new parents. "Congratulations!" I said. "She signed!"

I heard shouts of joy: "Hallelujah!"

"I'm coming up to the hospital now," I told them, to more excited exclamations.

In the hospital elevator I pushed the button for the third floor and marveled that it had been only four days since I had come to see Vicky and the baby. The nurse showed me to the "family room," where the new mommy, daddy, and grandma sat basking in the joy of their new family member. Daddy held Gracie, a smile of gratitude and love lighting his face. We all hugged and wiped back tears of joy.

They asked me to hold Gracie for a photo. She

felt so light and soft, and again my throat grew tight. A tear fell as I smiled for the camera. I carefully handed Gracie to her mama. Wordlessly, lest my voice crack and my emotions escape, I quickly signed the hospital forms. I handed the release papers to the social worker, and I left, hurrying down the hallway, into the elevator, and out the doors into daylight.

Five years earlier, I had left those doors carrying my own pink bundle. Now, my arms felt strangely empty. I pictured Vicky leaving the hospital and Li Hang's mother leaving the orphanage with aching hearts and empty arms, each leaving behind such beautiful gifts.

I ran to my car in tears, opened my purse, pulled out the small photo, and whispered, "Mama's coming, Li Hang. *May yo gwan she.*"

—*Pamela K. Amlung*

All names have been changed to protect the privacy of the people in this story.

My Whirling Girl

When Lily was a fish swimming in me, I imagined her as a boy, pounding away on a piano, growing up to be an artist like me.

She came out a girl. And she had the gene for rhythm, like her grandfather, who was a drummer. From the time she could move her hands, she would drum, and shake a rattle, and smile, and keep time to music.

But not just to music. One day while I was putting clothes in the washer, she crawled up to the machine, pulled herself to standing, and with wide-eyed anticipation, waited for me to shut the lid and turn it on. When the water started pouring in, she began to dance—a slight, tentative shaking of the hips at first. But by the time the machine was agitating the clothes, she was wild with the rhythm, bouncing from her knees and singing a long, joyful "Waaaaah" to the music.

I do not know why I imagined her as a boy. Perhaps I was afraid to see so much of me reflected in her: My eyes, which are my father's eyes. My sensitivity to people who come too close too soon. My fears that she could be hurt, as I had been, so young.

A boy child would have been easier. He would have been my husband's shadow, rather than mine.

When I found out I was having a girl, my stepfather said he'd known it all along. "You've done too much feminist crap to get a boy. This will be your chance to put in action what you've theorized."

He was right.

My twelve-year-old stepdaughter, Laura, plays the violin after dinner in the living room. Lily, not yet walking, sits next to her in rapt attention. At the end of the song, she cries, "WaWa!", her name for Laura, and claps.

Two days later, while we are driving around town doing errands, the *William Tell Overture* comes on the radio.

"WaWa!" Lily exclaims from the backseat.

This is the same piece Laura was practicing that evening.

Since Lily's birth, I have lived in constant surprise at her intelligence and joy. It is as if she knows something I haven't figured out yet or have forgotten, and this knowledge brings her profound happiness. I wonder how I've managed to pass this love of rhythm and music to her—I, who cannot carry a tune or keep a beat or play a note. How I could give birth to someone who looks so much like me but who is so different? I can only attribute this as a gift from something larger, from the goddess.

We are at a small women's gathering, Lily and I, a going-away party for a woman with whom I used to teach writing and yoga workshops. We are eating bread and cheese and carob-covered strawberries on blankets in a backyard, and talking, as women do, about food and our families, travel and our bodies, when suddenly from down the street we hear a horrendous noise: A neighbor has started up his chainsaw and is cutting wood. We can barely hear each other over the roaring. I turn and see Lily at the fence. She is bobbing up and down to the rhythm of the motor. Smiling. She hears the beat in everything.

There is an ancient Egyptian term for what our mothers give us in the womb: *ab*. It means "heart-soul"—a gift from the heart of one's mother.

As a verb, the word means "to dance."

One morning, as I prepare to get Lily dressed for school, I ask her, "Would you like to hear some music?" and head over to the tape player in her room. "Wawa-wa," she answers. "Wawa-wa." This, I realize, is her word for music—the name for her sister, but with an extra syllable.

Music is a sister to her, a great sister.

It is said that, unlike God, who speaks and puts the Word before everything else, Goddess does not speak, but dances, drums, and sings.

One day when I go to pick up Lily from school, I find all the kids and teachers in her class sitting on the floor while she dances for them. The music is a baby reggae tape, and she shakes, bobs, marches, whoops, laughs, and claps as she ecstatically performs for her audience.

When I pick her up to go, I hear a teacher say to another, "There goes our entertainment."

It is a kind of ritual my daughter does with her body when she dances. Those in her presence smile, and laugh, and come closer together.

Our word *religion* comes from *religare*, which means "to bind." Lily's birth binds us to one another—my husband, my stepdaughter, and me—as our families become one through her blood. Even my husband's ex-wife becomes a relation, as we become mothers to sisters after the baby's birth.

It is a kind of worship I do as I care for her. I am a mother to this great and holy being, full of joy and wonder, both my creation and yet so far beyond me, so much more.

Midweek, early evening, we look at the clock. Dinner is done, and Lily won't be sleepy for at least another hour. Sometimes parenting is a matter of killing time. Meili, my husband, decides to put on a record, a nice, slow piano sonata, something we haven't played since Lily's birth.

When the music starts, Lily gets up from her pile of books and walks over to the stereo. She stares at it, then slowly moves toward the middle of the room. She raises one arm in the air, puts the other over her heart, and begins to turn. Her left foot stays in place while her right leg pivots around and around.

She has never danced this way before.

We look at each other, amazed, as she spins, completing revolution after revolution.

Preparing for a lecture on Assia Djebar's *Fantasia*, a story of the relation between love and rape and colonialism in Algeria, I am reading a history of Islam. There, I find a description of the "whirling dervish," with one arm outstretched and one arm to the heart or the earth, as the dancer spins faster and faster into ecstasy. This rapture leads to the realization that there is no reality but God. We are all, then, potentially divine, as the self joyously unites with the universe.

Just so, I unite with my daughter, and with my husband, and with my stepdaughter and her mother—all family. And my daughter's presence opens my eyes to my past, to the pain that had for so long blinded me from seeing real joy. And in giving my love to Lily—my gift from my heart, from my blood—I begin to feel a constant, steady beat that has survived and goes on, that will keep on going on, long after I am gone.

—*Cassie Premo Steele*

 # From a Mother

I used to hate my knees. As a gangly teen, I thought that they jutted out from my slender legs like the backs of two fat, bald heads.

When I complained to my mother, she smiled and said, "You've got my knees. My brothers used to tease me about them until I'd cry."

I shot an alarmed glance at my own brother, but he hadn't been paying attention. He lay on the orange sofa, entranced by a television program.

I turned back to my mother and saw her like I never had before. Suddenly, the raised mole on the back of her neck was distasteful, just like, I then realized, the one on my upper arm.

"What else did you give me?" I accused.

"Well, let's see," she said, her eyes lit with amusement. She cupped my chin and gently tilted my head to the side to see my profile. "You've got my straight nose that ends in a ball." She tugged on my chin as if it were a goatee. "And look at that; you've got my witch's chin."

"Thanks a lot, Mom!"

"When you kids were babies, I'd lie down on my back with you right here." She gestured to her chest. "And you'd suck on my chin."

"Gross!"

"You didn't think it was gross then." She pulled me close, her grip on my shoulder tightening as I squirmed in a halfhearted effort to break away. "You have a better personality than me," she continued. "And instead of the one dimple that makes my face lopsided, you've got the perfect two to frame your sweet smile." She kissed my cheek.

"Mom!" All indignant teenager, overreacting, I wrenched free of her embrace. But as I walked away in an exaggerated huff, warmth melted away my teen angst. I was loved.

In my room, I tried on clothes. Fortunately, skirts in both midi and maxi length were in, so at least my fat knees were easily concealed. But what about my nose and chin? I tugged back my hair and used a hand mirror to examine my profile. My nose looked okay, but my chin did jut out a little like a witch's. I let my thick, straight hair fall back down around my face. And for the next two decades, I wore it just that way.

Years later, long past my teenage insecurity, I now

witness similar uncertainty in my thirteen-year-old daughter. She stands at the wardrobe mirror, trying to wrestle her thick, shiny hair into an elastic band. Uttering a grunt of frustration, she lets it fall.

"I hate my hair," she says. "It's too big."

I smile. "You got your hair from me."

She turns to look at me, reminding me of that long-ago conversation. "What else did you give me?" I hear her ask, although only her eyes speak.

"You're beautiful, Hilary," I say. "Someday you'll realize how wonderful your hair is."

At forty-one, my own hair is still healthy and thick, but not as much as it used to be. Thankfully, things like hair and moles and the size of my knees are no longer all-important. Other concerns take precedence, like making the most out of every day in this fleeting life.

Later in the afternoon, I sit on the garden swing, swaying softly. I'm wearing shorts, and the warm sun shines down on my bare knees. I'm missing my mother, remembering her pleasantly, yet grieving her sudden death as if it happened yesterday, not ten years ago.

Proving the soulful connection unique to mothers and children, my solitude is soon lost to my daughter. She joins me, quietly at first, as if tiptoeing around my mood. She sits silently on the sun-warmed cushion beside me. Contented to have her near, I draw my legs up beneath me and let my daughter do the swinging work.

After a moment, she leans her head on my shoulder, and we sit quietly, cuddling for a few moments. As she runs her index finger over the raised mole on my upper arm, the years melt away. She used to do that for comfort when she was small. I think of my mother's mole, just like mine only on the back of her neck. I used to look at it when we sat in church, at the way it stuck out in the soft strip of skin between her blouse collar and the wispy hairs escaping from her French twist. My mother would wrestle her thick locks up the way my daughter wrestles hers into a ponytail.

Pulling away, Hilary says, "Momma . . . I'm glad I've got your hair. Remember my friend Angel? She says she'd die to have hair like mine."

"That's because it's beautiful," I say, as I stroke the silky, light-brown strands cascading in a thick blanket down around her shoulders. The sunlight causes glints of spun gold and fiery red to jump from its lustrous depth.

"What else do I have of yours?" she asks.

I look down at her knees and try to imagine them the way she might see them—like fat, bald heads jutting from slender legs. But I don't see or say that. And although her face is shaped like mine, I don't see a witch's chin, either. For that matter, I don't see my physical features as faults anymore. They're just the concrete proof of inherited genes and a gentle reminder of the mother I miss every day.

My daughter runs her finger along the bottom of my bare foot. "You have alligator skin," she says and gives me the gross look. "You need lotion, Mom."

I laugh, thinking of my mother all those years ago, saying she had a ball on the end of her nose. Of all the things my mother gave me, the most important is probably a sense of humor—that, and the ability to make a daughter feel loved.

"And you have the cutest dimples," I say, tugging gently on Hilary's witch chin.

—Sheri McGregor

Grammy and the Dream Keeper

I tipped the dream keeper upside down, and the dreams poured out.

That fall afternoon, my daughter's third-grade Girl Scout troop had discussed the importance of dreams and goals. After our discussion, the girls, eyes wide, had fallen silent when I'd pulled out a brightly decorated can.

"This, girls, is a dream keeper. I want each of you to write one special dream that you want to accomplish this year on a slip of paper and deposit it in the dream keeper. We'll try to make every dream come true, and in spring we'll open the dream keeper and see how many we've accomplished."

Now with their dreams scattered before me, fear of disappointing the girls filled me with doubt. And I recalled the first time I'd become aware of the importance of dreams, so many autumns ago.

"Join me for a cup?" my mother had asked.

Happy, as always, to spend time with her, I settled into the chair next to her for one of our girl talks. But when I looked into the cup she gave me, I didn't see the weak tea I'd expected. This drink was red and opaque, yet somehow familiar.

"Tomato soup," she said.

"In a cup?" In all my five years, I had seen soup only in a bowl.

"Sure," she laughed.

"The color of our soup reminds me of a song," she said. Seated at our tiny dinette table, she sang "Scarlet Ribbons," about a little girl who wishes for scarlet ribbons for her hair, and though her anguished parent has no money to buy them, ribbons miraculously appear one night on the girl's pillow.

"Hold on to your dreams, honey," she'd said afterward with a smile.

"I will, Mama."

And I had. I'd attended college, married a wonderful man, taught elementary school students, and given birth to a sweet little girl of my own.

But during the two years that cancer had consumed my mother and the three years since her death, sadness had gripped my spirit and believing in dreams had become nearly impossible for me to do. I prayed every day for strength to smile for the sake of my daughter. Nina had been only five when she'd lost her beloved Grammy, who had never tired of hearing Nina's imaginary stories and who could make a trip to the drugstore seem like a trip to the moon. Shortly before her illness, she had taken Nina to her first state fair.

"And Mama, Grammy and I had corn dogs!" Nina exclaimed on her return. I never bought corn dogs, but my daughter and my mother both loved them.

One day just before Nina started third grade, she patted my hand. "I will be sad, too, someday when I miss my mama."

It hit me then that I had been sad most of Nina's life. I had to change. For my daughter's sake and my own, I had to learn to believe in dreams again.

Now, with the Girl Scouts' dreams scattered before me, I worried that I'd let them, and my daughter, down.

I fixed myself a steaming cup of tomato soup. And as I sipped the broth, I gathered my courage and confidence. I could almost hear my mother say: *Hold on to your dreams, honey.*

I picked up the first slip of paper. Sarah had written, "Go horseback riding." I sighed with relief. The girls, I predicted, would vote to earn the Horse Lovers badge, which included horseback riding.

Gillian had written, "Go to an amusement park." Great! Marine World had an annual Girl Scout day, and our cookie proceeds could fund that.

Corinne had written, "Go camping." I loved camping and would be happy to lead a trip.

Rachel had written, "Get a kitten." That would be a little trickier, but I'd show her the Pet Care badge. Her parents loved animals and would (I sus-pected) agree to her dream.

More girls dreamed of horseback riding, camping, and Marine World—so far, so good.

I stared anxiously at the last slip before me, the one I most longed and most dreaded to read: my daughter's.

With a child's faith, Nina believed that dreams come true. Not long after a skating accident that was followed by months of body casts and surgeries, she'd set her heart on running a local race. Despite her pain, she'd reached the finish line with a huge smile.

Crazy about sports, she had begun talking daily— a year in advance—of the Summer Olympics. "Wouldn't it be fun to go, Mom?"

"Sure would, sweetie." Unfortunately, the Olympics would be 3,000 miles away, a trip I knew we couldn't afford.

Fingering the last slip, holding my little girl's dream, I breathed deeply. Slowly I unfolded the paper.

Nina's writing was dark and firm: "Go to the Olympics." I stifled a groan. My daughter's was the only dream I couldn't help deliver.

That night I lay awake in bed pondering how I could show Nina that dreams are worth holding on to, even though I was having a hard time believing it myself.

The next day during dinner I said, "I love your dream. And I bet that someday you will go to the Olympics. But we can't afford that kind of trip this year. So, instead, why don't we go see the torch-bearers when they run through town, watch the games on television, and look for articles about the Olympics in the paper?"

It was all I could think to do. Would she feel that the dream keeper was nothing but a lie and that I had let her down?

She paused for a moment, and then she beamed. "Thanks, Mom! Doing those things will be great!"

Admiration for her good heart washed over me.

Months passed, and Nina continued talking daily about the Olympics, delighted at watching the torch-bearers run through town, and collected articles on her favorite athletes.

One evening at dinner she mentioned, "When I'm at the Olympics . . ."

I put down my fork. Had she misunderstood all along? "You understand, don't you, that we can't attend the Olympics?"

"You said we can't *afford* to go, not that we *can't* go."

"What?"

"We can go if we can afford the trip, right?"

"Well, I guess so, but how—"

"I'm earning money and praying about it," she said matter-of-factly.

I exchanged concerned glances with my husband but said nothing. Neither of us could bear to squash her dream.

Nina took on as many odd jobs as she could find—no job was too big or too little. Though I admired her faith, I worried about when our troop would open the dream keeper at the end of the school year and find that all the girls' dreams had come true—except Nina's.

At the grocery store one day, Nina dashed up the soup aisle. "Mom! Come look!" She led me to the refrigerated meats and pointed to a display featuring the Olympics logo. "It's a contest," I said, tearing off an entry form. "Adults enter by mail, and the winner and a guest go to the Olympics."

"Yes!" Nina sliced the air with a victory punch.

When we got home, I set the entry on my desk, put away groceries, and made dinner. By the time I'd washed dishes, packed Nina's lunch for the next day, and checked her homework, I'd forgotten all about the entry, which was already buried under the day's mail.

Weeks later, Nina asked, "Will you bring Daddy or me as your guest?"

She was referring, of course, to the entry, which

I'd long forgotten. My stomach lurched. Had I missed the deadline?

"Who do you think, silly? It's your dream. But as I explained before, our chances of being chosen are slim."

"But we have a chance!" Yes, we did.

As soon as she bounced from the room, I excavated the entry from the mountain of paper on my desk. Mercifully, the deadline was still days away. She and I can fill it out together tomorrow, I thought. Or will I forget again? I filled out the form, but at the sound of pounding rain, I had second thoughts. Go out in this rain? The odds of winning are so slim, it's just a waste of a stamp. Nina assumes I mailed it. She'll never know the difference.

The dream keeper sat nearby, watching. *Hold on to your dreams*, I could hear Mom say.

I pulled on my raincoat, walked to the mailbox, and pushed the envelope through the slot. At least she and I would both know that we had done what we could to make her dream come true.

The other Girl Scouts, meanwhile, set goals and achieved their dreams, one by one. We camped, rode horses, and visited Marine World, and Rachel got a kitten. Nina continued saving her money, collecting news clips about the Olympics, and occasionally asking if I'd heard anything about the contest.

With our last troop meeting approaching, it was clear that Nina would miss attending the Olympics.

But she was satisfied with what she had done, and seeing the girls' joy and enthusiasm while accomplishing their dreams had rekindled my faith in the power of dreams.

As I stepped outside our house one spring morning, I nearly tripped over a fat envelope on our doorstep. I tore it open and read:

> Dear Ms. Doherty:
>
> Congratulations! We are pleased to inform you that you and your guest have been selected to attend as our guests at the upcoming Summer Olympics . . .

The sponsoring company would host six days, five nights, meals, hotel, travel, and seven Olympic events!

I called to Nina, "Want to join me for a cup?"

I poured tomato soup into two mugs and told her the news. She let loose a howl of pure glee.

"To Grandma!" I held up my cup for a toast. "I bet she's watching."

Nina grinned, clinking her cup to mine.

We spent six glorious days at the Olympics. Whether Nina's dream came true by luck or design, we don't know. But we have a suspicion. Our host, a company called State Fair, makes only one food: corn dogs.

—Marla Doherty

Before the Rain Comes

I read my mother's diary when I was twenty-two. Of all the summer days that I was home from college, I'll never forget that June day. My parents were moving, and it was my job to clean out the attic. While I was sorting through a box labeled "college papers," I saw nestled between heaps of yellow papers a dusty gray book adorned with a white stripe. I know I shouldn't have, but when I flipped it open, I saw my name and couldn't put the journal down.

October 16, 1974
... Catherine is here. We just got back from the hospital yesterday. What a happy day! My beautiful baby girl is here and asleep in her crib. She is so precious. She's a gift from God! I'm happy and I'm sad. I'm just so tired. There are so many things to do now. I hope I will be a good mother. I don't know if I can give her all the attention

that she deserves. Lord, please forgive me for what I almost did. How could I ever have considered that? I'm so glad I ran into that little girl and her mother that day. I will make it up to her. She will be my sweet baby girl and I swear on my life here and now that I will do everything I can to make sure that she grows up happy. . . .

I slammed the book shut. Dust flew into my face, but I didn't bother to wipe my eyes. I couldn't move. Considered what? Who did she run into that day? What was she talking about? I knew what it was, but still I read that paragraph over and over again, until I couldn't see the words anymore. I forced myself to continue, this time from the beginning.

March 27, 1974
. . . I'm pregnant. It feels so weird to write this down. My aunt cried and hugged me when I told her in the waiting room. She said she'd let me tell my parents. Good God, what am I going to do? I can't have a child! I can't tell my parents, they will surely flip. I have to call Tina.

March 29, 1974
. . . I haven't been able to sleep. My face is breaking out and I feel like a walking zombie. I stood in front of the mirror today and pressed my T-shirt against my belly. It stood out slightly, but hopefully only I can tell. How can I tell my parents? I'd have to go to confession every

day for the rest of my life. I can barely take care of myself, let alone anyone else. I just can't handle that kind of responsibility. I mean, I'm only fifteen. Stupid, stupid boys. Tom said this wouldn't happen. What did he know? When would I finish school? Everyone would make fun of me. I just got elected secretary of my class for next year! By then I'd be fat and obviously pregnant. I just can't imagine my life without school, without basketball games and pep rallies, without Mr. Darling in English class, without Friday night parties at the old playground. It's not fair. It's not my time! I'm going to have to do it. I'm just not ready to be a mother. I couldn't handle it. I guess I will ask Tina to make the appointment. Yes, I have to. Please forgive me, but I have been over and over this in my mind and I just have no other options. . . .

I let the book slide off my lap. My throat hurt, and I was dizzy. The sun had almost disappeared, but through the dirty window I could make out a blackbird sitting on top of the yellow swingset my dad had made for us kids. Seeing the bird caused me to think of the nursery rhyme my mom said I'd loved: "Hush little baby, don't say a word, mamma's gonna buy you a mockingbird. And if that mockingbird don't sing, mamma's gonna buy you a diamond ring. . . . " I imagined her at sixteen, a baby herself, standing there holding me and humming that song.

My mother was always humming. I remember her humming while cooking breakfast, while cutting lilacs and arranging them in a vase, while walking past the open window with iced tea in her hand, while driving us to school or driving the family to church. It was a soft pleasant hum, like the mockingbird song. To this day, when I hear someone hum it puts me at ease.

March 30, 1974

. . . Tina just called. It was not easy to get the appointment, but somehow she managed to do it. Yesterday, I tried to call the clinic but I hung up each time someone answered the phone. All of a sudden I just couldn't speak. It's at three P.M. on Saturday and Tina is going to drive me. I know she doesn't want to but she is a good friend. . . .

April 2, 1974

. . . I still can't sleep. I dream of children. Last night I dreamt that I was in a park watching a little blond girl fly a kite with her mother. She was dressed like me, in blue shorts and an orange tank top. They were both laughing and looked so happy. Suddenly I heard a car honk behind me so I turned my head to look. A few seconds later I turned back but the girl and mother were gone. All I could see was a red kite alone in the blue sky. . . .

The sound of a car skidding to a stop jarred me back to the present moment. I looked out the smudged window but could see only the lightning bugs blinking in the dark backyard. The yard hadn't changed much since we were kids. The concrete basketball court, swing set, and monkey bars my dad had built were still there. My eyes fell on a flattened basketball in the center of the white concrete. That was where I found my last clue for the scavenger hunt we'd held on my eighth birthday. A note was taped to the basketball that said, "Where does the family go to be warm in the winter?" I went into the living room and there stood a five-foot-tall dollhouse on wheels. The front looked like a real yellow house with a brown door. My parents wheeled it around and revealed a living room, kitchen, two bedrooms, two bathrooms, and an attic. The floors were carpeted; the little wooden stairs and furniture were carved in great detail; the lights worked in all the rooms.

"Your dad and I built this for you," my mom had said, grinning like a little kid.

April 6, 1974
. . . The day is here and I'm glad. I just want to get this over with. No one is home. Mom and Dad are golfing as usual. Wait! I hear Tina's car. Gotta go now . . .

April 8, 1974
. . . Saturday was insane. I remember every detail.

Tina's green Chevy was parked across the street. As I walked down the front steps, I remember thinking that the sun hurt my eyes even though it was cloudy. I got in the car and she stared at me like I was someone she didn't know. "What?" I asked as I looked in my purse for my matches.

"Well," she said, "for one, you look like—"

"Shut up," I interrupted.

"Fine," she said and pulled away from the curb. We were silent the rest of the way. She pulled up to the front of the clinic a few minutes later. "Here we are me-lady," she said cheerfully. I couldn't believe she was acting like she was dropping me off at a party. Then, in a shaky voice, she said, "Are you sure you want to do this?" I knew I'd cry if I said anything, so I just jumped out without saying a word.

I watched Tina drive away. Some part of me hoped she would turn around and come back. Another part of me wished the day were already over. Still looking in the direction her car went, I walked toward the building's steps. Deep breaths, deep breaths, I said to myself. This is no big deal, just a simple, standard procedure. Tom doesn't need to know. No one else needs to know.

I couldn't bring myself to look at the building. I felt like I was going crazy. Kids were everywhere—in the cars driving by, on the playground across the street, walking along the sidewalk with their parents, in strollers, on bikes. Everyone was hurrying to get out of the wind and the approaching storm. I set my purse down, cupped a cigarette with my hand, and lit it. My throat was so dry it tasted awful. As I stepped forward to toss it into a trashcan, I tripped over my purse and stumbled across the sidewalk. I hit something hard and heard a woman cry out. Then I felt pain in my knee. I looked toward the grass between the sidewalk and road and saw a little blond girl looking at me. She had a bit of grass in her hair and I realized I must have knocked her over. "Are you okay?" I asked, with a small smile. She had a shocked look on her face, so I wasn't sure if she was going to cry. All of a sudden she let out this sweet high-pitched laugh. It seemed to echo down the street and back again. She looked at me with her big blue eyes and clamped her hand over her mouth. I busted out laughing. She let out a delighted squeal, which made me laugh even louder. I just sat there on the grass laughing while the wind blew my hair in my face. I felt my shoulders start to relax, and for a moment I forgot where I was. I hadn't made anyone laugh like that in a long time and it felt great. I reached up to push the hair out of my face and saw the girl's mother out of the corner of my eye. She wasn't paying any attention to us. She was looking at the clinic. She met my gaze and I looked away quickly. I felt ashamed and she knew why. "My daughter likes you," she said softly.

"You'll make a good mother someday." She looked at the building and back at me again. "You'd better get home now before the rain comes." I didn't say anything; I just stared at the few strands of grass on my jeans. "Say good-bye," she said to her daughter. The little girl waved, turned, and skipped down the sidewalk. Her mother followed after her. I watched them until they disappeared around the corner.

"Why am I here?" I said out loud to the deserted street. "This is crazy. I can't do this." Yes, I thought, I do need to go home now. . . .

I heard someone humming below me. "Where's my sweet baby girl?" my mother called up the stairs.

"I'm here, Mom," I said. I wanted to run down the stairs and tell her that I knew what she went through and that it was okay. At the same time, I wanted to make her feel bad, to punish her for almost going through with it. But I knew I would have done the same thing had it happened to me.

"Are you about finished up there?"

"Yes, I'll be down in a few minutes."

I heard humming again and then the sound of the door closing. I wiped my eyes and looked down at the dusty gray diary on my lap. It was as much a part of my history as it was hers, so I decided to keep it. Maybe someday I'll tell her, I thought to myself.

—Catherine Olson

My Mother's Hands

From my earliest memories, I can plainly see my mother's hands. Skin soft and warm as velvet, the olive complexion a gift from her Cherokee grandmother. Fingers, long and slender, forever in motion, punctuating, decorating, creating a visual image to accentuate her spoken words. My father frequently claimed that if her hands were tied behind her back, my mother would be unable to utter a single sound. This statement was always followed by his rumbling laughter and my mother's playful slap to his shoulder. Growing up, I often wondered whether he'd ever put his theory to the test.

Imagine, if you will, the activity in a household of six free-spirited children—the quarrels, the laughter, the wrestling matches that brought down my mother's favorite table. The time my sisters and I persuaded our three brothers to be our cosmetic "guinea pigs." To this day my youngest brother has an aversion to a particular shade of berry-red lipstick, which I fail to understand completely. At the time, it looked quite becoming on him.

There were birthday parties and homecomings, first dates and last dates, broken toys and broken hearts, weddings, births, funerals, practical jokes, and tears. Through it all, bringing every tragedy back full circle to laughter and love, was the guiding influence of my mother's hands. Mending. Smoothing. Comforting. Calming. Always reaching out to touch the face, the hair, the forearm of one of her six children. Relaying through a simple touch, the message: grow strong, grow happy . . . I am here behind you; you will not fall.

As a child, I would lay my head in the welcoming lap of my mother and drift into a blissful, dreaming sleep as those gentle fingers stroked and combed the dark locks of hair tangled from a long, tiring day of childish adventures.

The years have trickled by. We all grew, married, gave her grandchildren and then great-grandchildren. My mother is happiest when in the midst of her family. She was surrounded by her children when the news came of the tumor nestled between her lungs—cancerous and inoperable. I have never been more proud of my mother than I was on that day. Her hands lay still in her lap; fingers I once believed never rested were calm, without movement. She faced the doctors and the diagnosis with a fortitude I've never seen in another.

My mother is still with us. During the five-year battle for her life, she has never questioned the "why" of it. She has yet to shed a tear in self-pity.

I was with her one night recently. We sat quietly together, she and I. She was sitting up in bed covered with an afghan her mother had made for her before I was born. And, once more, I laid my head in the welcoming lap of my mother and felt those gentle fingers stroke and comb the dark locks of her child's hair. My tears came softly as the child within the adult tried in vain to come to grips with the mortality of one so beloved.

My mother placed one of her hands next to mine and said softly . . ."Look, honey, you have my hands."

—*Patty Briles*

The Circle Plant

My dear friend Bernice and I became close friends when we were both newlyweds and lived with our husbands in the same apartment complex. When Bernice gave birth to Tessa, I gave her a dish garden to celebrate the beginning of her new daughter's life. The live plants, I believed, would brighten her home and last much longer than a floral arrangement. A rose-colored violet and a shiny pink bow set off the dark green, heart-shaped foliage of a *pothos* plant. Bernice loved my gift, and baby Tessa was fond of the shiny pink bow. Over the years, as our friendship and families grew, so did the plants in her dish garden.

Our daughters Tessa and Corrin and Laura and Tonya played together and had pajama parties at each other's homes. As the years have passed and we've raised our daughters, together Bernice and I have shared the trials and joys of being moms, surviving diapers, kindergarten, junior high, first dates, proms, and everything in between. All too soon, our daughters were grown.

After my eldest daughter, Laura, married, through a coincidental series of events, she and her husband purchased the home right next door to my friend Bernice. As a special house-warming gift, Bernice potted up some of her sixteen-year-old *pothos* plant from that original dish garden and presented it to Laura. Laura treasured the plant and placed it upon a shelf in her dining room, where it thrived.

For my fiftieth birthday, Laura gave me some wonderful presents. One gift, though, was more meaningful than all the rest. Laura had taken cuttings from the pothos plant that Bernice had given her and placed them in a handpainted clay container. That beautiful plant, originally given to celebrate the birth of my friend's daughter, had traveled a loving circle back to me.

Bernice's younger daughter, Tessa, is now an athletic high school senior, planning for college and her future. My youngest daughter, Corrin, has her own sweet little baby girl, Alyssa, who loves to toddle over to my plant and touch the glossy foliage. There must be something magical in those heart-shaped leaves.

Like our precious daughters, our plant has flourished and given us years of enjoyment. It symbolizes the loving circle of life. Tonya, Bernice's older daughter, will be married this fall. To celebrate another new beginning—the life she will share with her husband—I am giving to Tonya something old, yet new. Something special and priceless. A sprig of her mother's circle plant.

—*Susan J. Siersma*

 # Fashion Amnesia

I am clueless about teenage fashion. It's a genetic flaw, inherited from my mother, who lost her sense of style when I was thirteen.

Frustrated by failure, I don't buy clothes for my daughter unless she is with me. Emily's dramatic eye-rolls and deep sighs guide me as I try to trigger my faulty memory.

"Hey, this is cute. Do you like this shirt?"

"Yes, Mom, that's cute, but I wouldn't wear it. You always pick white shirts. They're so bo-or-ring."

"But it goes with everything. What about this one?"

"Oh, Mom." Emily shakes her head at me. "It's hopeless, you don't know fashion."

The current problem is that Emily's "perfect" jeans shrunk. She needs an outfit for a dance tomorrow, but can't shop with me. Nervous and alone, I enter dangerous territory for a fashion amnesiac.

In the juniors department of Burdines, surrounded by neon colors and heart-pulsing bass music, I review what I know. Jeans should be flared, the center front and back of the legs should be faded, and the waist should be hip-hugger.

I begin my search with a rack of Levi's. They are dark blue and barely flared. Emily would never wear them. I move to a headless Lucite mannequin, naked except for pants. "Super sexy, bikini-cut, neo-flared, gotta have 'em jeans" is scribbled in magenta on a yellow plastic rectangle chained to a belt loop. Metallic sparkles woven into the denim feel like sandpaper. I choose not to buy "super sexy, bikini-cut" jeans for my daughter.

By a mirrored wall of tiny, cropped tops is a display of pants similar to Emily's shrunken pair. I check details. Leg flare, hip-hugger, faded pale blue in the right places. I grab a pair and hug them to my chest. They're perfect.

Inspired, I select a purple tank top with tiny beads along the neckline and a white three-quarter-sleeve shirt with lettuce edges for Emily. I choose a periwinkle cardigan and matching turtleneck shell for me, pleased that my outfit is from the juniors department, too.

The cashier is a slender girl with funky dark-rimmed glasses and maroon tousled hair. "Oh, I love this tank." She gently refolds the purple shirt on the

counter. She's trained to compliment customers' purchases, but I want to believe her. "It is so-o-o-o cute."

"Really? I'm glad you like it. It's for my daughter."

"How old is she?"

"Fifteen."

"Well, I'm eighteen, and I like it."

"Good. That's a relief."

My fashion consultant/cashier relishes her
authority. She scans the white shirt's barcode. "This
is good, too. I'd wear it." She nods approval and pats
it with her navy blue fingernails.

"Good." I stand straighter, confident I can master
teenage fashion at forty.

"Uh-oh. Well. Ahhh, I don't know about this
one," she warns as she picks up the cardigan. She
holds it like a dirty rag.

I think, But I picked it out in this loud, hip,
trendy juniors department! Aloud I mumble, "That's
okay, that one is for me." I drop my head and stare at
the pink-and-orange carpet, afraid to meet her dis-
approving gaze.

"Well, the turtleneck is alright. I guess."

Maybe I still have a chance. I lean toward her
and desperately wave my arm at the last item. The
reason I'm here.

"How about the jeans?"

I'm a grown woman begging fashion advice from a
young stranger. I feel vulnerable, like a peer-pressured,

acceptance-hungry adolescent. I realize how important these jeans are. They have to be right—for my memory and Emily's dance.

I fidget and wait for the cashier's verdict. She hesitates. She looks down her pixie nose at the folded denim. Her head tilts as she considers them. "Well . . . "

I don't breathe.

"Are they flared?" she demands, one hand on her stylish hip.

"Yes. Yes, they are flared." I answer like cornered prey.

"That's good. 'Cause if they're flared, that's good. Even bootcut is okay. But straight cut, relaxed fit—that's the worst." She snaps the pants open and holds them in the air for final review. Her eyebrows disappear under her bangs. "Wait!"

I wait.

"Hey, these really are hot!"

"Really?" I start to jump but stop myself. I want to hug her. I grin and pay my bill.

A surprised Emily loves her new jeans and purple tank top. I bask in the success I know may not come again. Emily doesn't love the white shirt, but that's okay. It's perfect with my black, relaxed-fit, straight-leg Levi's.

—Karen Favo Walsh

The Birthday Promise

Today, as promised, Mother, we're going to spend some quality time together.

I awoke at 5:45 A.M., as you had done for so many years. I put on your tattered bathrobe that I thought I had discarded. I was pleased I hadn't, because your favorite scent, Tabu, still permeates its fibers. I stuffed my feet into your slippers and was glad that they were open in the front to accommodate my longer toes. Now, we're together again. At least it feels that way to me.

It's been a very long year, Mom, and I miss you so much. But I'm doing okay. Well, I'm trying, and you always told me that's what counts.

I know you enjoyed an early breakfast, and I've got all your favorites. Most of the world drinks coffee or tea in the morning. You drank soda: "Coke-a-Cola," as you called it. You told me it was a Southern custom. I never believed that for a moment, even though you were born and raised in Virginia. I think you needed a sugar high to start the day. It was a tough choice, but I decided on the peanut butter crackers for the main course—handmade, not the packaged ones, spread one at a time straight from the jar and pressed together like an Oreo cookie.

The birds have started to sing outside, and the sun is announcing the beginning of another new day. Right about now, you would have turned on your radio and tuned into your favorite radio station. Here goes! . . . Guess what? They're playing one of your favorite songs, "That Old Black Magic."

Peanut butter isn't all that bad in the morning! Do you remember when you used to feed my German shepherd peanut butter crackers? How she loved you for that! The peanut butter would get stuck to the roof of her mouth and made her look like she was smiling. You always had such a way with animals.

That brings to mind the time my beloved parakeet, Buckey Bird, flew into the frying pan while you were cooking breakfast. I wasn't supposed to let him out of his cage, but I had, and he burned his feet. I thought you'd be so mad at me, but all you could think about was getting medical attention for that poor bird. The pharmacist thought you were nuts when you asked what brand of antibiotic cream he would recommend to rub on a parakeet's feet.

Speaking of funny animal stories, do you recall when my pet hamster, Brownie, got stuck in the dryer hose? You called Sears, where you'd purchased the clothes dryer, to ask how we might get him out of the predicament. They told you to turn on the machine, and the initial thrust of air would push him through. We did, and Brownie the Hamster Cannonball flew through the air. Daddy caught him in his baseball glove. It was hard to believe, but the exploding hamster lived to see another day!

Which reminds me . . . do you recollect the time I blew up the stove while trying to earn my Girl Scout cooking badge? It took a year for my eyebrows and eyelashes to grow back. You slept with me that night and told me that it wasn't my fault. Still, it was a long time before you left me alone in the kitchen.

I never told you this before, but after my baking fiasco, your own dear mother shared with me a secret about the pressure cooker she'd given you as a wedding gift. The first time you used it, you'd set the timer to "high" and your chicken dinner became part of the kitchen light fixture. Grandma told me it took Daddy a week to scrape it off the ceiling. At least I only lost facial hair.

Your mother must not have criticized you, because you never lectured or punished me for all the foolish things I did through the years. You said that everything was a learning experience and that as a child I had an active imagination and marched to my own drummer.

I think I'm still that way, Mom. And that is exactly what I try to focus on when your two granddaughters are yanking my chain. They're doing fine, but they miss you. Both of them keep a photo of you in their living rooms. The great-grandchildren, all five of them, will never forget their "Nana Virginia."

You were always so proud of my girls. You never missed a chance to tell me what a good job I was doing in bringing them up. I want you to know how much your saying that meant to me and that I couldn't have done it without you.

Your granddaughters both have your tenderness and your tenacity. I remember the time the oldest one decided to run away from home. She announced over dinner that she was leaving to go live with her grandparents, six blocks away, because I was much "too mean." I wanted to lock the kid in her room. You suggested that I let her work it out on her own, that it would be a learning experience. She packed such a heavy suitcase, she made it just three blocks before she collapsed in front of the neighborhood bakery. The owner drove her home in the bread truck and gave her a dozen doughnuts. He still looks at me in a funny way.

Mom, do you think the lesson she learned that day was to always pack light when traveling a distance? It worked, though. She was too tired to recall why she was angry and too full of jelly doughnuts to care.

Recently, your other granddaughter was looking at all the pictures you'd taken when the two of you had traveled together. I'd forgotten how many countries you'd visited over the years. I do remember, like it was yesterday, the call I got saying that you had to cut short your Hawaiian vacation because you'd been hit by a surfboard on the beach at Waikiki and received twenty stitches in your leg. Your granddaughter stayed up all night and tended to your needs. In the morning, she made all the flight arrangements to get you home. She was only thirteen years old. You were so proud of her.

I know that feeling today, Mom, when I see what wonderful mothers my daughters have become.

As for your great-grandchildren, all I can say is that they have an overabundance of energy; either that, or I'm getting old. A photo of the entire family sits on my dresser. Everyone looks so happy. We still are. I thought you'd like to hear that. It's difficult without you, but I think we're finally getting our act together.

It's getting late, so I'm going to put away your things for now. We'll do this again next year, promise.

Happy birthday, Mom.

—Anne Carter

 Leaving

The first time I left my mother, I was five years old. She told me I couldn't go out to play until I picked up my toys. Who could tolerate such treatment?

"I'm running away," I announced.

"Oh, dear, I'll miss you," she said, shaking her head, "But if you really want to go, I guess I shouldn't stop you."

Mother got my red coat from the closet and tucked my white mittens in a pocket. "You'd better wear these," she said, "It's just mid-afternoon and already chilly out there. It will get really cold tonight."

She walked me to the porch, kissed me good-bye, and closed the door behind me. I heard the deadbolt slide into place.

Off I stomped. As I passed the house next door, my

footsteps slowed. It struck me for the first time that I had no idea where I was headed, and after a moment, I turned around. Plopping down on our front steps, I began to consider my immediate future. But as the afternoon wore on, I didn't stir from my spot.

Mrs. Ford, our neighbor, took out her trash and called, "Hi, honey. How you doing?"

"I'm running away," I said, and my lips started to tremble.

"You are? Well, I won't disturb you then," she said, and went back inside.

As darkness fell, I decided to be generous. I knocked on the door, and when Mother opened it, I strolled past her.

"I'm giving you another chance," I said, as she wrapped me in a warm hug.

"May I have a kiss then?" she asked.

Not yet totally forgiving, I replied, "My kisses haven't come in today."

"I love you," she said, "Come on, the meatloaf's already on the table."

After supper, I climbed into her lap and covered her face with kisses.

"They just came in," I explained.

"I'm so glad," she said, "Now, go pick up your toys."

I never ran away again.

But I left, and that's different. First, I left for the

first grade. I didn't have far to go, because our house was just across the street from my school. On the first day, I ran home at lunch, barely able to contain my excitement. "Mom! You'll never guess what happened. I can read, 'I can run'!" I shouted.

She enveloped me in a hug. "That's wonderful!" she said, "I can't wait to see what you'll learn this afternoon."

I hurried back to school. I couldn't wait to find out either.

Next, I left for college. She waved until my train pulled out of sight. She had helped me pack my bag, and when I got to my destination, I found a note she had tucked among my sweaters that read, "We're so proud of you!"

Though I was beginning to grow up and to break away, when I was lonely, I could phone to hear her voice. Our conversations always ended with, "I love you." The mail brought boxes of peanut butter cookies she had baked, clothes she had made for me, letters full of news from home.

When I married, I left again and moved far away. She remained my touchstone. At first, I phoned to ask trivial things: "Mom, how do you bake that chocolate cake with fudge icing?" She wrote out the recipe and sent it.

Then, I phoned to sob out the news that broke my heart: "Mom, I lost the baby." She came the next day.

Finally, I phoned with words I dreaded to say: "Mom, my marriage is over." She didn't pry, assigned no blame. She simply said, "I love you." I went home to my parents and got well inside.

Each time I left, she sent me off with a smile and words of encouragement. She never clung, though sometimes she couldn't hide the tears in her eyes.

I always felt her by my side.

Years went by, and in my thirties, I began law school. Then the day came when it was time to leave again. In the past, leaving had been a matter of choice, a part of getting on with our lives. Not this time. Before, we'd always known we'd see each other again soon. Not this time. I had always been the one who left. Not this time.

Mother died ten days after she was diagnosed with cancer. It was not an easy death, but in the midst of pain, she managed to tell me one more time, "I love you."

I went on living, because that's what people do. Each morning, I got out of bed and did whatever was necessary. I returned to law school classes, with the bittersweet knowledge that, though I would soon become an attorney, my mother would not be there to share the day when my dream came true. Friends helped. Work helped. But I moved mechanically through my routines. For the first time in my life, I could not sense my mother by my side.

One evening, as I was going through her things, I found a quotation she had written in the margin of a book: "Love is a very agreeable passion, and sometimes it is stronger than death." She believed that, and I had the feeling she had written it for me to find one day, after she'd gone. And I realized it was true. Mother had never really left. The way she'd lived her life remains as my moral compass.

Born to privilege, she hadn't complained when her fortunes changed, but had simply dug in and found ways to keep her family happy and secure. During the Great Depression, she'd tried to stretch our food each day to save a little for tomorrow. Yet, when those with no food came to our door, she'd made sandwiches for them. With grace, she'd played the hand that was dealt her. Poverty, war, the loss of my dad, and cancer: she'd faced them all and managed to find joy, despite them. Her faith had never wavered.

I see her smile in my memory. I hear the echo of her thoughts in my own. I find her love when I love others. I feel Mother always by my side. And I know this: Love is a very agreeable passion, and sometimes it is stronger than death.

—Ramona John

The Comforter

"I have made you at least five comforters, Liz. And there's not a one in sight when I'm chilly." Mother feigns sternness, but her voice is shaky, the cruelty of body parts carrying no lifetime guarantee.

"Ah, but there's never one far away." I laugh and head for the den. I return, arms full of cornflower blue and mauve patches, and tuck the quilt around her knees. "To make up for the inconvenience, I'll include a cup of coffee absolutely free of charge."

"That's more like it," Mom says and chuckles.

I bring each of us a steaming mug. She grasps hers with both hands, attempting to get cup to lips before tremors betray her.

At that instant, the thought strikes me: I've just tucked her in and brought her a drink. When did we switch roles? When did I become mother, and mother become child? Did it happen gradually or as suddenly as it seems?

A cascade of memories floods my mind: When new skates throw me to the sidewalk, Mom is immediately there, applying kisses and tape to my scraped knees and soothing words and hugs to my damaged pride. Sitting tucked beside Mom on our old flowered sofa as she drilled me on words from the third-grade speller. Mom loosening my braids and guiding my awkward hands as I attempted to wind reluctant locks around a plastic curler. Mom admonishing me through a mouthful of pins to hold still while I fidgeted and twirled in my first formal dress.

"Your white daisies are lovely." Mom reaches out to touch a bright yellow flower, part of an arrangement on the coffee table.

"They're yellow daisies, Mom, not white," I say in a low voice, not sure I want her to hear. Not sure I want her to realize that the girl who once blushed in her first long dress is now correcting the creator of that dress in identifying the color of a flower. It is, after all, an unimportant detail that cataract-glazed eyes can no longer discern.

"They look as though they could use a little water." Mother dips one finger into the vase and pulls it back dry.

I set down my coffee cup. Over the knot in my throat, I manage, "I've been so involved at the school's Clothes Closet, sorting donations for the fall sale—" I pick up the vase and escape to the kitchen.

"You and your projects," Mom calls after me with another chuckle.

Old memories gurgle up like the fresh water bubbling to the top of the vase. . . .

As I piled bulging suitcases and a one-eyed teddy bear into the family car, Mother stood in the doorway with my younger brother and sister. I waved, and already missing my room's yellow-flowered wallpaper and Mom's goodnight kisses, I ran back for one more teary farewell hug, while Dad waited in the car. Her return hug was followed by a gentle swat on the seat of my jeans.

"Go on," she'd said, "I've spent too much money on foot-lockers and popcorn poppers to have you back out of college now."

Suddenly, I picture in my mind's eye the red-white-and-blue quilt. While I wrote heady letters home expounding on my all-important causes, my newly acquired knowledge, and my freshly formulated opinions, Mother sent praise and encouragement. One such letter was tucked among the folds of a lap-size red-white-and-blue quilt of her own creation.

A few years later, the red-white-and-blue quilt and I moved into our own apartment, furnished with a love seat and kitchen table bought on credit.

Mother congratulated, lined shelves, and co-signed.

Then came that special Fourth of July when fireworks exploded—between Christopher and me. I rushed home with my husband-to-be in tow. Did I see Mom's shoulders droop slightly? Did a hint of a wrinkle cross her face? But the wrinkle quickly rearranged into a smile. The shoulders squared. And Mom's arms enfolded us, as she rejoiced with me, her child in love.

The water spills over the top of the vase and across my hands. I turn off the faucet, grab a towel, wipe down the green ceramic, and return to the living room to set the flowers on the table.

"Mom, remember when I used to call home sniffling about marital spats and strained budgets?" I suddenly realize I speak to her in louder tones these days.

"Yes, yes." She smiles. "I think I threatened to lock the door if you tried to come home."

"No, you didn't. But you did place a hand on each of my shoulders, like you always did when you were about to say something profound, and said, 'Liz, making a marriage is like making a comforter.' I thought, wow, she's flipped for sure. Then you said something I've never forgotten. You said, 'You and Christopher are beginning with a collection of separate pieces of cloth, all different colors and shapes. You must arrange them into a pattern. You'll try them one way, and if that doesn't work, you must try another. With patience, eventually you'll come up with a whole new pattern, a unique design all your own that has never before existed.' You were absolutely right!"

"Well, wasn't I quite the guru, though?" She laughs.

I stand, give her a hug, and pick up our empty cups. At the kitchen doorway, I stop and turn to say, "I'll tell you this, guru, there were some days when that design was a little too unique. Days when I was ready to throw out the whole damn bag of scraps."

I leave her laughing and go to the coffeemaker.

As I refill our coffee cups, I think about the good laughs and good times that came after those early marriage-making days. Was I still the child when I went to Mom on sun-drenched summer days, babies in tow? Together, she and I had giggled at the antics of toddlers and at my belated introduction to the real art of quilting. We exchanged favorite books and secret hopes. We hadn't yet exchanged places.

And there was the tissue thing. Like some intuitive wizard, Mother always magically produced a tissue from a sleeve or a pocket when tears erupted or a nose dripped. But then there was that day she and I were huddled in a hospital room, dreading the sound of the gurney that would whisk her away for surgery. That time, it was I who offered Mom a hankie and assurance. Was it then that we traded places?

Or was it much later, when her aching back or her swollen, arthritic knees kept her on the couch all day? I presented her with my first comforter about that time, an imperfect burgundy and rose reproduction of one of her masterpieces. It was also during that period that often, over her protests, I'd tidy up the stacked dishes in her kitchen.

"Liz, dear, you do too much. You have a family to see to. Just leave the dishes. I'll be fine in the morning."

I chose not to notice that things wouldn't always be fine in the morning. I glided through the days, the years, careful not to look too closely at the toll that time was taking on my mother, willing life to remain the same. Mom would always be there, I assured myself, to teach, to sew, to tend, to make my hurts better.

But the mother who once shooed me off to college now clings to a farewell hug, though I live just blocks away. Now, I'm the one who drives the car, opens the door, and carries the packages; the one who advises and encourages, soothes and pampers, supports and praises.

How did this transformation come about? Perhaps it is the work of a makeup artist—a jokester flaunting a sober sense of humor who has sprayed her chestnut hair silver, perched eyeglasses on a smooth face made corrugated, stuffed cotton in unsuspecting ears.

"Liz," Mom calls.

My daydreams scatter, and I return to set down cups of fresh coffee.

"Someone is coming to the door, dear." She wears a mysterious smile.

I catch a glimpse of movement through the window. It's Sara, my daughter, running up the walk, clutching the hand of a young man. Pausing at the hall mirror, I brush back a straying gray curl, square drooping shoulders, and reach for the door.

—B. J. Bateman

Pearls

Around her neck my mother wore a necklace: a string of jaggedly spherical luminous beads. I don't know why she chose that necklace for that night. Her sister's wedding, perhaps, called for the touch of a family heirloom, or maybe she simply liked the way it sat above her collarbone in a path of smooth stones. All the same, it was on that night that she chose to wear it—this favorite piece of hers—a gift from her late grandmother.

On my mother's lap I sat in a curl—no older than seven, with little patience for adults or conversation or wedding parties. With my ear to her breast, her voice reverberated as though echoing out of a dim cave in the wells of her chest.

My mother's boyfriend was tall and lanky. He had a reddish face, and his ears looked as though they had been pinched by the lobes and stretched out an extra inch. His eyes were gentle, but I had no taste for men who were not my father. I was too shy to accept his numerous offers to dance, while my mother eased naturally in and out of conversation with the other women at the table.

"She's living in Corpus now."

"That's right. She married an optometrist, didn't she?"

"Charlie Campbell."

The band music, the women's voices, and the vibration of my mother's chest, had all begun to blend into a lulling rhythm as I stared at the old women on the makeshift dance floor waltzing with their sons. Between my right fingers were entwined the jewels that settled around my mother's neck, spiraled around the small of my hand, twisting effortlessly, the cool stones rolling over my fingertips, sliding across my palm, tightening at her throat.

Had my evening ended like that, the entire memory would have been lost in the pile of my past, like any other childhood moment. But it did not. In a snap as quiet as the sound of a pin popping through fabric, my mother's necklace unleashed from her throat, a ripple of beads falling to the floor like rain. She gasped, pushing me from her lap, leaving me wide-eyed and mesmerized by the glittering pellets that rolled and hopped off the carpet, some even reeling their way to the hard edge of the dance floor.

Under the table, past the chair legs, she and her boyfriend bent over desperately plucking the shimmering orbs from the floor and filling their hands with them.

My mother never spoke a word of that night in my presence. I was not scolded or punished. Instead, I watched her eyes build a thin glassy layer that she would not allow to form into tears. Days later I watched her try to string the gems back together— new thread, fewer beads—a sort of concentrated muteness drawn over her features. A reproach in itself, the meticulous movement her fingers made leading the needle through the tiny, clear holes. A lesson that could not have been learned from scolding: here, the actual ache of guilt in my stomach. A lesson in my mother's silence and in that image of cascading beads, a shower of crystalline globes, like tears from the caverns of her chest.

—*Martha Lackritz*

"Pearls" was first published in *Prospect: An Anthology of Creative Nonfiction*, Spring 2000, Brown University.

My Funny Mother

My mother speaks what I call cliché speak. Whatever the trial or tribulation, the difficulty or the heartbreak, my mother can always be counted on to come up with the perfect cliché to heal the wounds and soothe the heart.

I love my mother's clichés. Indeed, I call her at those moments when I am most in need of one of her comforting and oddly wise one-liners. She never lets me down.

"He doesn't want to be married anymore, Mom. He just doesn't want to be married," I sobbed over the phone.

"If he can't take the heat, he should get out of the kitchen."

"I don't know if I can ever fall in love again. How can I ever trust another man?"

"Pat, when you strike out, you just have to get up

and bat again."

"He says he needs to 'find himself.'"

"Tell him to look under his hair."

And I felt better.

In a less-enlightened time, I worked as the only female in a department of males.

"They rig up the reels so that I get shocked when I touch them."

"They sound like real big, brave men to me."

"They tell the boss if I'm late or make a mistake."

"They want you to be 'job-scared.'"

"Gary locked me in a high-voltage cage, Ma. He thought it was funny," I complained.

"Tell him he'll think it's funny when it's on *60 Minutes*."

Just like that, she'd sent me back to the work world, madder than hell and wondering how to contact Morley Safer.

My mother can be a godsend when it comes to my own parenting challenges.

"She drives me crazy, Mom. She lies about being sick. She steals from me. She tells her grandmother that I spend her social security money." I relay the latest antics of my teenage daughter.

"Maybe you should write a book and call it *Daughter Dearest*."

"She told five different lies to five different people. We compared notes."

"You can fool some of the people some of the time. . . ."

"Now, I don't know when she is really sick or just faking."

"There *is* something going around."

Somehow, in just a few phrases, my mother convinced me that my daughter *is* a problem, that I am *not* crazy, and that she might *really* be sick. And she'd given me the confidence, clarity, and calmness to deal with it.

My mother used to be a beautiful woman. Even now, in her seventies, she is handsome. She was once hired to "swoon" for Frank Sinatra during an appearance at Baltimore's Hippodrome Theater. Though she has never had a "career" of any sort, she has been employed as a waitress and a barmaid and was once hired to model an iron lung.

Mom has given birth to seven children: three by one man, three by another, and one whom she gave up for adoption. We are all reasonably intelligent and not unattractive—except the adopted sister, who is extremely skinny and a crazy Elvis fan. We've all given her smart, attractive grandchildren.

When we argue, as mothers and children naturally do, she brings it to an immediate halt with the statement: "Don't ever forget. I'm the one who laid down and had you."

We all readily accept her eccentricities. She refuses to drive at night, ever. She never changes the route she drives, no matter how many expressways and byways they build. If the route changes—say, if a lane is added to one of "her" roads—she simply stops going to whatever place that route had taken her.

She does, I admit, do some strange things. The unkind would call them silly. The kind would call them unique, like the time she was following me to an unfamiliar destination.

"Just stay behind me, Mom. I know right where we're going."

"Let's get behind the wheel, McNeal."

We did fine . . . until we got to the tollbooth.

It was a normal tollbooth, the kind with several drive-through areas in which to pay the tolls. During non–rush hours, several lanes are usually open and waiting for customers. Such was the case the day my mother was driving behind me to New Jersey . . . and ended up in Pennsylvania.

The problem began at the tollbooths.

Because I had only a five-dollar bill for a one-dollar toll, I decided not to enter the "exact change only" booth, and within a split second, immediately realized the folly of my decision. I kept my eyes glued to my rear-view mirror and willed my mother to pull in behind me. Please, God, don't let my mother have exact change, I thought, knowing that, if she did, she would believe it mandatory to go through the exact-change lane. And if she entered a different booth from mine, she might pull out ahead of me, and, well . . . my mother gets confused sometimes.

My mother had exact change.

I watched in dismay as she pulled into the exact-change lane, tossed in her coins, and—while the collector counted back my change I'd given him—took off. By the time I exited the tollbooth, she was out of sight and headed in the wrong direction. I had to search every exit and make countless U-turns, and it took more than an hour, but I found her.

I'm not sure why, but my mother goes into high hysteria whenever she cannot reach me immediately on the telephone. Her phone messages could be transcribed and submitted as comedy sketches.

"Pat, this is Mom. Listen, I really need to talk to you. Call me. Mom."

"Pat, please call me. Every time I call, I get this answering machine. Mom."

"Pat, this is Mom. Look, I don't know why you don't call me. I really need to talk with you. Mom."

"It seems like all I ever talk to is this answering machine. If I ever die, I told Ernie not to call you, to just drive down and tell you your mother is dead. Call me. Mom."

"Pat, look, I've got something really important to

tell you. Listen, it's really, really important. Call me." Followed by the consecutive message: "Pat, I forgot to tell you who I was in the last message. This is Mom."

And so I call.

"Hi, Pat," she says. "Listen, I have a confession to make. I don't have anything important to tell you. But I knew it would make you call."

What can I do but laugh and settle in for a chat with Mom?

In my middle years, I decided to pursue a writing career. My mother doesn't read, at least to my knowledge, and I don't recall ever being encouraged to read as a child. In fact, she would often admonish me for reading too much. My mother has yet to read a word I've written, though she has often been the wellspring of many of my fictional characters. Yet, she wholeheartedly supports my passion for the written word. Though she doesn't understand anything about writing or the publishing world, she dutifully told all of her friends that her daughter had written a book.

She'd rather hear, than read, the tales of murder and romance that I weave. So, I spend hours on the phone, telling her my stories. She laughs and cries and gasps in surprise, just as though she were reading them. She listens raptly as I talk about plots and protagonists and bylines.

When one of my short stories was finally published, I thought, Now, my mother will read something I've written.

"It's in *Birds and Blooms*, Ma. You can buy it in a magazine store."

"A magazine store? Oh, yeah. I think we have one in Columbia."

"I can order one for you."

"No, that's all right. I'll have Michael pick it up for me. No, wait, he's on vacation. I'll go myself. *Birds and* what?"

I knew it was hopeless. Finding a store that carried small specialty magazines and remembering the title of the one my story had been published in were beyond my mother's ken. I ordered her a copy from the publisher.

When I made it into a large publication that I thought even my mother was familiar with, I was sure my mother would at last read my work.

"*Reader's Digest*, Ma. You know, *Reader's Digest*. You don't have to go to a special magazine store. You can buy it at the supermarket."

"I think Ernie used to subscribe to that."

On the other end of the phone line, I rolled my eyes to heaven. She hadn't heard of even *Reader's Digest?*

I realized then that my mother would never actually read anything I'd ever write and that I would have to be content with telling her my stories. Still, this news was too good to keep to myself.

"*Reader's Digest* is distributed worldwide. It's an excellent opportunity. Of course, my piece is only two sentences, but . . . I don't care what it takes, Ma, I'm going to write for a living, even if the only book I ever publish is a payroll manual. I'm going to succeed at this."

"I have no doubt that you will."

I stopped still. The phone line crackled.

"You really believe that?" I asked. After all, most of my "success" talk was just a pep talk to myself. Other folks in my circle usually acknowledged such comments with a nod, if at all. Now, here was my mother, who'd never read a thing I'd written, much less anything else, saying with firm confidence that she had no doubt I would succeed as a writer.

"I wouldn't say it if I didn't believe it."

And I knew it was true. If she disagreed, she might say nothing. But my mother never said anything disingenuous, that she did not wholly believe.

My mother believes in me. Whether I succeed or fail, I will forever have that knowledge. I won't let her down.

—*Patricia Fish*

Lava Love

She was my mother—and more. We were best friends. It had nothing to do with the years she spent grandmothering my two children. It was more than our early-morning conversations about stocks and bonds as I sipped coffee and watched her cook biscuits and Southern gravy. Our friendship extended beyond the family gossip we rehashed each time we were together, as if we were telling those stories for the first time. Ours was a friendship of quiet, silent, absolute love. It simply was. Like the oceans, pine trees, and lava rock, it needed no reason.

Mother was a mover of mountains. Literally. Each summer, at our mountain cabin, she loaded three rambunctious dogs into a Toyota four-by-four and bumped over rugged roads up mountain slopes. Heavy gray cowhide workman's gloves protected her tiny hands as she loaded up piles of sharp black lava rock, careful to leave small spaces around the rocks inside the vehicle for her dogs.

At home again, three dogs tumbled out of the Toyota while Mother headed for the kitchen. She would open the fridge, pop the tab on an ice-cold can of Miller Lite, and walk outside to survey the next section of wall to be raised. Year by year, stone by stone, she built a low wall of dark, rich rock stacked around the wide circular driveway.

Mother matched her persistence with an equal measure of patience. She was in no hurry. Moving rocks allowed her to enjoy brisk sunny days in the mountains. It gave her an excuse to tour back roads with her dogs, and it provided a reason to reward her exertions with cold beer. Why hurry?

If she could push and tug rocks into position with fierce determination, she could also coax a number-ten short needle through a plump quilt with the greatest of finesse. What delightful hours we spent together bent over a black nine-patch quilt, sewing and discussing ways to make our stitches even and tiny. We never hurried. Running small stitches along seam lines was simply our excuse for passing time together in constructive, quiet contemplation.

I never worried about Mother. When my father died of lung cancer brought on by forty-five years of smoking, she showed us the stuff of which she was made. She nursed Daddy at home until his death. I went with her to the mortuary to make arrangements for his cremation, but a week later, when I asked about returning to the mortuary with her to pick up his ashes, she told me not to worry. Coming home with Daddy was something she preferred to do on her own.

Friends suggested that she settle close to her children, but Mother would have nothing to do with that idea. Daddy was gone, but she wasn't. And she was determined to live her best life. Within the year, Mother sold the family home my father had designed twenty-five years earlier and relocated to the country. She was ready to move on. Regrets were useless, if there were any. She never said. She simply knew what she must do.

During her years as a widow, at five o'clock every morning, with the sun still below the rise of the hill, Mother put on her swimsuit in 40-degree weather and drove through the darkness to the community pool for water aerobics. A tremendous cook and proud of her vegetable garden, she was always ready at a moment's notice to whip up a delectable stir-fry. With her own mother approaching ninety, the future looked bright.

I certainly didn't expect her to be struck overnight with a brain tumor. Cancer knocked her feet out from under her and made her an instant invalid. Confused about the order of pills and meals she needed to follow, and unable to read her stock reports, she came to depend on us for every personal need. Good fortune provided a leave from my teaching job, and I threw myself into every moment of Mother's day, grateful to be useful and to be sharing her final months. We cried together for the first few days. But as in all things we had shared in the past, we knew when to move forward. I moved into Mother's home and became her cook, nurse, accountant, advocate, priest, chauffeur, scribe, and aide. She always showed appreciation for the Malt-O-Meal I prepared to her taste and for my managing to hit the proper ratios of instant coffee and cream.

Even the hardest of experiences gave us reason to celebrate. What a victory it was when she and I found a way to lift her off of the low couch where she spent the day! We squeezed into a tight bear hug, with her toes resting on my feet and our faces pressed tightly together, which allowed me to swing her into her wheelchair—an adventure that always ended with giggles and salutes.

I chased down medications and learned nursing duties I never thought myself capable of. In the daily routine that evolved, I watched the direction of the fan we had placed in the room, making sure it cooled her without chilling her; kept the radio tuned to a soothing station; opened and closed window blinds as each day brightened and darkened; learned her favorite evening television shows; and made sure we went outside on the patio as often as possible. When Mother was no longer able to speak, I sat by her bedside waiting for those infrequent moments when she would open her eyes and I could smile a hello to her. And finally, one early morning, with a faint pink halo outlining the mountains outside the window and Mother lying in my arms, I shared her final breath. She was gone.

After the first busy days of change, silence settled in. In my despair at having to go on without Mother, walking through the silence of her empty house, I faced the same loneliness I now knew she experienced during her five years of widowhood. Unexpectedly, regrets surfaced, taking control, breaking through the secure love I had never questioned until now. How many lonely nights after Daddy's death had Mother suffered in silence? How many times had I called to receive her comfort during my personal trials, unaware of her own need for comfort? Were the last four months I'd spent at her bedside truly an act of selfless dedication? Only now, reflecting alone upon those months, did I have the courage to admit that sitting at her bedside was what I had needed. Had Mother really wanted privacy? Had I been too much in her face?

Regrets attacked my memories of even the simplest acts of love. Over and over I'd told her, "I love you." Over and over my voice conveyed the sense of loss I felt. One morning, in a burst of final effort,

Mother inhaled enough air to expel a forceful, "I love you," her reassurance to me. But it wasn't enough. I hung on. How I wished I'd been able to rest in the quiet certainty of the love that had surrounded me for more than forty years.

And some regrets are just too much to handle. On her final morning, Mother opened her eyes in terror, overhearing the nurse tell me she would make the trip to the pharmacy for the morphine. Mother knew morphine. She knew it marked the final stage of the same journey through cancer she had shared with my father as his nurse, a journey she was repeating in every detail as my patient. I promised her, "Mother, I won't give you morphine unless I ask you and you say it's okay." Her eyes softened with gratitude, and we sat in silence.

How was I to know I would have to break that promise within twelve hours? Where were the doctors and nurses at midnight when I really needed them? Why did I have to be alone to decide? But I was. I took her hand and whispered, "Mother, squeeze my hand if you can answer me." In despair, I waited. I knew I would have to do what I never thought I could: give Mother the medicine that would take her away from me forever. In the darkness, I leaned in to her ear. "Mother, you can't squeeze my hand. Please forgive me. I can't bear to see you hurt anymore. I don't know what else to do.

I wish you could tell me, but you can't. I love you."

The nurses who came later used all of their experience to tell me I had done the right thing. But that didn't stop my regrets.

Life without her wasn't easy, a succession of empty spots where quilting and bear hugs used to be. But as Mother taught me, time moves on and so must we. The family cabin in the mountains needed painting, and when neighbors called to inform us that fierce March winds had removed a row of shingles, I packed the van and headed north.

As I pulled into the drive, I surveyed the lava-rock wall. No happy dogs ran up to greet me, no call from the kitchen door invited me in for Miller time. I looked up to the roof and counted the bare spots where shingles had broken loose, making a mental note of additional needed repairs: bird holes at the upstairs window, a broken antenna, and wood sorely in need of paint.

I looked down to the ground. Old, dead sunflower pods lay there, soggy in the patches of melting snow. Stepping from the car, I followed the sunflower trail along the lava wall and collected the pods to dry. I stopped. There at my feet was a lonely lava rock. I bent down to set it back on the wall. But the rock tottered. The wall had settled into a crooked list, and I knew it wouldn't have met with Mother's approval. I knew she would have insisted on removing this section of the wall to rebuild it properly.

I dropped to my knees. The breeze brushed against my cheeks. Down with the rocks and up again, I matched each jagged lava edge to form a straight vertical line, saving the tiniest rock for last. It would fill a small gap to make the top of the wall flat. As I reached for the final rock, a sharp gust of wind caught some sand and sprayed it across my face. I blinked, and tears washed away the fine grains. In the hush of the crisp mountain air, my hair sailing across my face, I heard my mother's voice. Quiet, sure, and filled with love, she spoke to me:

"Jane, it's all right. You did the only thing you could do." A tear fell on my knee, making a dark-blue circle on my jeans. "You did your best. You did everything you could." And in that moment, my heart shifted like the lava rocks my mother had tugged into place in her wall, and I left regrets behind.

The wind quieted down. A bluebird sailed across the drive, landing in a low juniper bush. He cocked his head and watched as I reached once again for the last lava rock. Carefully, I put it in its place. My hand rested on the top of the wall, feeling the cracks with the tips of my fingers. I was still on my knees as the light breeze began again, and my eyes followed the curve of the low wall as I bowed my head in thanks.

—Jane Tod Jimenez

The Demise of Josephine

"Mom—mm—mee!" The shriek pierced the air.

I groaned, forcibly more than half awake now. It could only be Rachel, her voice distinguished by the permanent note of panic she'd seemed to acquire since turning twelve. I opened one eye. Directly in my line of vision, about two inches from my nose, my daughter held out her hand, flat, palm up. Dismay shot through me, waking me immediately and completely.

Was that Josephine lying in Rachel's hand? I sat up to get a better look. Yes, it was Josephine. She lay stretched on her side, her little paws curled under, her beady eyes slightly opened, her tiny rodent teeth exposed.

"What's wrong with her?" Rachel asked, but her face told me she already knew. She just wanted me to tell her it wasn't true.

I touched Josephine's golden blond fur with one finger. The little body felt cold and stiff.

"She's dead," I blurted out before thinking to soften the words.

Rachel gasped. "She can't be!" She let out a cry, then covered her face with one hand and with the other offered up the deceased hamster as if it were a grief offering.

"What happened?" I asked, leaning over to examine the remains more closely. Mercifully, the corpse wasn't mangled, nor was there any blood. In fact, Josephine looked as if she might be napping— except that, of course, golden hamsters normally sleep curled tightly in a furry, warm ball.

"By the way, where is Garfield?" I asked abruptly.

Rachel shrugged her delicate shoulders. Then her eyes widened with suspicion as the same thought occurred to her.

Garfield chose that moment to saunter into the room, his entrance heralded by loud intimate purring. He wrapped his body lovingly around one of Rachel's ankles. She jerked back. Garfield had been her darling since he'd come to live with us three days earlier. Now, she shrank from him as if he were contaminated.

Resigned to the fact that my day had definitely started, I hugged Rachel, dead hamster and all, and tried to reassure her. "Look, honey, why don't you wrap Josephine in a tissue . . . "—I yanked one from the nightstand—"and I'll find a nice box." I kissed her cheek. "Okay?"

"Okay," she said meekly, standing motionless, holding the hamster, the white tissue draped like a shroud.

Rushing through the den, I almost fell over four-year-old Timothy, who sat in a trance in front of the television set. Later, I thought, streaking into the kitchen.

I stopped, stunned. My kitchen looked like a band of monkeys had used it for survival training. The remnants of my children's breakfast littered the entire room. A box of cereal spilled variegated color into milk puddles. A turned-over glass of juice dripped orange raindrops onto the floor with the rhythm of Chinese water torture. On the floor in front of me, a banana made a lumpy spot with a perfect imprint of someone's big toe. I examined the bottom of my foot: my toe.

I closed my eyes. Count, I told myself. Remain calm. On the count of six, my eyes opened slightly. Hmm . . . If I squinted just right, the milk puddles became creamy paint, the effect soothingly cool and pure. The teaspoons transformed into stark slashes of blue-gray. The cereal became flecks of life force, vibrant colors of red, orange, and yellow. I had stayed up late the previous night, sketching, thinking, trying to capture an idea for my art class tonight. Now I knew what I would paint. My fingers itched for a stipple brush.

Instead, I picked up a cardboard container, noticing it held one donut with a bite taken out of it. The box pulled me back to my mission. I ate the donut and emptied the powdery sugar over the sink, covering the dirty dishes with fantasy snow. The cellophane window on the donut box lid crackled as I inspected the interior. Perfect.

"Mom, did you know Josephine is deader than a doornail?" asked Paul, my ten-year-old son, in his moms-are-slightly-deaf voice as he sauntered into the kitchen. "Wow! What happened?"

"That was my question," I said with some heat, finally having enough presence of mind to scrape up the banana before I stepped in it again.

Paul laughed. "Garfield, primo rodent killer, must like his milk and juice after a long hunt."

He pointed. Milky paw prints made a trail on the counter.

"I heard that," Rachel said hotly, walking toward us with measured steps, Josephine still in hand.

Timothy, perhaps sensing a show more compelling than his television program, followed close behind.

"I know how Garfield did it," Paul announced with a smug undertone. We all turned to him, riveted in spite of ourselves. "I found Tim's door open this morning."

Rachel moaned. Technically, Josephine belonged to Rachel, but I had moved the cage into Tim's room when Garfield had seemed too intrigued by hamster smell.

"That cage was in pieces all over the floor." Paul gestured with hands, playing his audience well. "Cedar shavings, food, poop—everywhere."

"Did not! Did not!" Tim piped up, stomping his legs in a little dance of protest.

I knelt down and held Tim's wiggling body. "It's okay." Then I kissed him under his ear, his favorite spot, and he relaxed against me. "Did you have enough breakfast?"

Tim's hazel eyes, so much like my mother's, were somber. "Oh, Mom," he pleaded as he seized my face, held it between his small palms, and placed his nose on mine. "Garfield didn't mean to. It was an accident."

"I know, big boy, it wasn't anyone's fault." I gave him a little squeeze.

I held out the box for Rachel, and she carefully slipped the hamster, tissue and all, into its coffin.

The sudden weight took me by surprise. Josephine had seemed almost weightless when she'd scampered across my hand or up my arm, her paws brushing against my skin like fairy wings. Now she felt like a very solid rock. For a split second, tears blurred my vision. I pushed down the hinged lid. No. I will not let myself get upset over a stupid hamster—a rodent, as Paul had pointed out.

I must have audibly sniffed, because my children stood staring at me with wonder.

"Go on . . . get ready for school. I'll get this cleaned up," I mumbled. The least I could do, I thought with a touch of remorse, for jumping to conclusions about the kitchen mess.

Rachel put Josephine's box under the sink.

"Mom, guard this with your life. We'll have the funeral after school," she said with a trace of anticipation in her voice.

Funerals at our house were a common, frequent, and strangely enjoyable family event. Anything that had once lived in our loving care deserved, we felt, a proper closing to its life. Actually, we buried everything, from roly-poly bugs washed to death inside of pockets to sidewalk kill, mostly earthworms and baby birds. Josephine's demise, however, was our biggest and most heartfelt since Paul's goldfish, a prized trophy from the school fair, had succumbed to fungus on its scales.

Hmmm, maybe I should add a touch of yellow ocher to the snow-white background of my new painting.

Later that day, I leaned toward the mirror to put on my new lipstick, Burnished Copper. I always took pains with my appearance for painting class, the one night I shed my role of housewife and mother as if it were a favorite old bathrobe I hung on a hook behind the door. I gave my hair a final pat and sprinted down the hall to the den. All three children sat in front of the television set.

"Dad's running late but should be home soon," I said, frantically searching for my purse among the sofa cushions, clothes, books, and papers. I looked at Rachel to make certain she'd heard me. "You should be all right," I said, with the slightest hint of a question in my voice. "Maxine is right across the street if you need anything."

Rachel looked up at me indignantly. "Mom-m-m, kids my age already baby-sit—for money."

"In your dreams," I replied, finally locating my purse under the ottoman. I grabbed my paint case and headed for the door.

"Wait!" The shout filled the entire room.

My heart thumped against my chest. Now what? I looked at the front door longingly.

Rachel shot up from the floor, eyes round and large. "We forgot about Josephine's funeral, a proper one with a service and . . ."

"Honey, I can't stay. My instructor takes only those who come for the first class; after that, enrollment is closed." I paused for this information to sink in. "Tonight is the first class, so I have to be there.

Can't we postpone this?"

"Better not," Paul broke in. "Out all day? Bet Josephine's kind of ripe."

"Ripe?" Rachel looked aghast at me.

"Never mind, Rachel," I said hastily. "Why don't you have it when your dad comes home? You know how he enjoys a good funeral with you kids."

"Can't." Paul again. "He has to take us to swim practice as soon as he gets home."

Silence.

Rachel stepped closer to me, her chin quivering slightly. She resembled a drooping daffodil, her blond hair covering her lowered face. "I forgot about Josephine's funeral. I got so busy, I didn't even think about her all day. Oh, Mom, I feel so-o-o horrible."

"I do, too," I had to admit. Sighing, I led her back to sit on the sofa with me. While I struggled to think of something that would soothe our mutual guilt, Timothy began to chant, "I want her alive . . . I want her alive." Large tears ran down his plump cheeks.

Something close to despair washed over me. I put my hand over my eyes. There goes my class.

At that moment, I heard my daughter murmur, "It's all right, Tim. Sister will take care of it." She put her arms around him and kissed him on his favorite spot.

Hope welled up in me like an underground spring rising to the surface.

"Mother, go to class. We'll have the funeral," Rachel said, sounding very grown-up indeed. "Paul can dig the hole. I'll do the service."

"Me, too." Tim jumped up and down.

"Sure, you can sing a song," my daughter said. "It'll be really nice. We can be finished by the time Dad gets home."

I couldn't believe it. Rachel was managing without me as if it were the most natural thing in the world. I felt as if I had accidentally flipped through a photo album of the future and had caught a glimpse of the woman she would one day be. Maybe I wasn't the only one needing a little room to grow.

"Rachel," I said warmly, "I think that's the greatest idea ever."

Reaching for the doorknob, I glanced back one more time. Rachel met my eyes, a hint of a Mona Lisa smile curving her lips. For that moment it was just the two of us, as if we were sharing some ancient secret. How very extraordinary, I thought, are the ordinary moments of love.

"Oh, by the way, Rachel," I said to her, glancing at Tim. "It's best to keep the service short." She nodded in understanding.

I opened the door, stepped through, and didn't look back.

—*Kristl Volk Franklin*

A Little Night Music

When I was a little girl, my mother sat on the edge of my bed every night and sang me to sleep in her soft alto voice. She sang lullabies and old folk songs, soothing melodies that eased me from wakefulness into slumber. Those peaceful few minutes at the end of the day are among my sweetest childhood memories.

I remember watching my mother and thinking how beautiful she was, with the light from the hall illuminating the curve of her cheek and glowing like a halo in her wavy hair. I wished the moment would never end, but no song lasts forever. I promised myself that when I had a daughter I would sing to her as long as she wanted.

I never forgot that promise. When my husband and I brought our long-awaited baby daughter, Tessa, home from China at the age of eleven months, I was ready. On our first night together at home, I held her across my lap in our big oak rocking chair and sang the familiar lullabies I had waited so long to sing: "Rock-a-Bye, Baby," "Twinkle, Twinkle, Little Star," and "Hush, Little Baby." I sang all seven verses of "Hush, Little Baby," which I had painstakingly memorized in preparation for the occasion.

When I had finished singing, Tessa wasn't quite asleep, but she looked drowsy. I rose and headed toward the crib to lay her down, but she immediately sat up and started to fuss. Okay, I thought, she needs a little more time. So I sat back down and sang the lullabies again, waiting for her eyes to close. They didn't. I sang my songs one more time, throwing in "The Alphabet Song" for good measure, until finally she seemed to be asleep. I laid her in the crib and turned to leave. Then I hit a squeaky floorboard. Tessa's little head popped up, and she began to wail.

When I had vowed that my child would get as many bedtime songs as she wanted, I hadn't counted on this particular child's determination. Perhaps, having waited so long for a family of her own, she didn't want to let me go that easily. And I couldn't bear to allow a child who had so recently left the orphanage to cry herself to sleep.

But I was quickly growing tired of the songs I had previously been so eager to sing. Tedium isn't necessarily a liability in a lullaby—it is possible to bore a child to sleep—but I found myself yearning for a little musical variety. I realized that it was going to take more than my tiny collection of lullabies to get my daughter to sleep.

In the months that followed, I tried out a variety of bedtime songs so that I could add the best ones to my repertoire. I evaluated each tune according to Tessa's personal rating system: She fussed and frowned when she didn't like a song, and commanded, "Again, Mama," when she did like one.

Not every song I auditioned made our lullaby hit parade. I like Gershwin tunes, but Tessa is no jazz baby, so "Embraceable You" didn't make the final cut. On the other hand, I found that cowboy songs make surprisingly effective lullabies. The lyrics are a bit melancholy, but the rolling rhythms of "Red River Valley," "I Ride an Old Paint," and "Down in the Valley" are soothing, like riding a gentle old pony into the sunset. Likewise, the sentimental songs that were popular early in the last century—"Good Night, Ladies," "Let Me Call You Sweetheart," and "You Are My Sunshine"—are still lovely, even when they're sung by a solo alto instead of a barbershop quartet.

And Tessa loved the folk songs my mother sang to me all those years ago, songs like "The Big Rock Candy Mountain," "I've Been Working on the Railroad," and Tessa's favorite, "The Riddle Song," which she immediately dubbed "The Cherry Song":

I gave my love a cherry that had no stone
I gave my love a chicken that had no bone
I gave my love a story that had no end
I gave my love a baby with no cryin'.

After eleven or twelve songs, Tessa would relax her hold on the day, her bright eyes would close, and I'd hear her breathing grow deep and regular. Carefully, I would lay her in her bed and creep from the room. We had triumphed over wakefulness for one more day.

This was our routine for many nights, until finally Tessa learned that when I left her in her bed, I wasn't leaving for long and that a cry of "Mama!" would always bring me back.

Tessa is six now, too big to hold across my lap, so I sing to her in bed. It no longer takes a dozen songs to get her to sleep; usually one is enough.

"What do you want me to sing tonight?" I ask, stroking her hair.

"'The Cherry Song,'" she always answers, with a sleepy smile. And I sing her that sweet song of unending love.

A cherry when it's bloomin', it has no stone
A chicken when it's pippin', it has no bone
The story of "I love you," it has no end
A baby when it's sleepin', there's no cryin'.

After she falls asleep, I linger a while. I sit on the edge of her bed thinking how beautiful she is, with the light from the hall illuminating the curve of her cheek and shining like a moonbeam on her sleek black hair. I wish the moment would never end, but no childhood lasts forever. And so I try to make memories that will.

—*Carrie Howard*

Mama's Egg

The furnace stopped the day my father died.
Much as she loved Dad, Mama seemed more
daunted by the loss of that nearly new furnace than
by the loss of her husband. I didn't understand that
at the time.

Many of the good people of Colfax, the small
Iowa town where my parents lived, were already
waiting at the house when Mama and I returned
from the hospital in Des Moines. Sad, sun-lined faces
came to cry with us. They brought nourishing food
and the gentle touch of gnarled hands. Throughout
the afternoon, their conversations rose and fell like
hilly country roads as they laughingly remembered a
cherished incident or sadly regretted the community's loss.

Then, as twilight edged across our small corner of
the world, mourners began to leave. They said,

"We'll miss John," and lowered their eyes. A dark-haired woman among them handed my mother a carton of eggs. Surprised, Mama looked back at her.

"In my religion, we believe the egg symbolizes life, Louise. You must eat one each day after you lose someone you love. It brings hope."

Mother smiled warmly as she hugged her friend goodnight. Finally, the last mourner had gone. Though we were grateful for all the kindness, we were ready to be alone. We needed to talk and to reassure each other.

"Are you ready for your egg, Patty?" my mother asked me.

I hated eggs, but knowing my mother's superstitions, I had to eat one. This newly found ritual might give her comfort. With messy shells in mind, I held my egg over the sink and cracked it.

"My God, Mom, it's raw!"

"You've got to eat it," Mama said, selecting one for herself.

Barely choking back nausea, I managed to swallow my egg. She ate one, too.

The next night, even my love for my mother, even my desire to support her, was not enough to endure one more raw egg. But true to her belief in hope, each evening Mama ate another . . . and another . . . and another, with the same gusto and devotion she gave to the novenas of her own faith.

We had spent much of my childhood alone together while Dad was away in the Navy. But resourceful and strong as my mother always was during those husbandless years, I never really saw her clearly until after my father's death. Perhaps that was because I had become a woman by then and better understood the harsh challenges of life.

We didn't speak of eggs again until several weeks after Dad's funeral, when Mama's friend asked, "By the way, Louise, did you eat the boiled eggs?"

The two of us exchanged amused glances and nodded, "Yes."

Boiled eggs? It didn't occur to us to cook them. That would have been too easy, and maintaining hope never is.

Death didn't stalk my family again for nine years.

During that time, Mama got a job. She made new friends. She quit smoking. She bought another house. She taught herself to play the guitar. She organized a bus trip for people from Colfax to go and see the pope when he came to Des Moines. She even spoke of finding a boyfriend, but opportunities were few.

My widowed mother lived a full life.

Then, too soon, the sad news. The phone call I had feared all my life came one night while I slept, warm in my husband's arms. It was unlike Mama to call so late.

"Patty, they've found a spot on my lungs." It had taken her many hours to summon the courage to tell me.

I listened quietly as she revealed the details. My body went cold. Now was the brittle time. Now was the time when nerves could shatter. I would have to be stronger than I had ever been.

Now was the time to cradle my mother.

I flew to Iowa.

The next day, after hours of agonizing, screaming grief, I returned to my mother's hospital room and sat on the edge of her bed. She had undergone surgery to see if the cancer had spread.

It had.

Looking at her solemn face, I asked, "Did they tell you, Mama?"

"They didn't need to. I knew it was bad when I woke up and you weren't here." She smiled gently.

I cried, feeling I had let her down.

She touched my face to comfort me. "You're gonna lose your mama."

"I know."

"Can you handle that?"

"Yes, Mama." I answered the hardest question of my life in a little girl's voice, unsure of my honesty.

My husband, Bill, had seen enough of hardship in his own life to understand my need to bring my mother home to live with us in Colorado. Fortunately, she also agreed to this move, since I, as her only child, would have full responsibility for her care. She left her home, her friends, her job, and as always, she did it with a light touch and a smile.

I thought I understood what it would take to help my mother face death, but I still had a few of her lessons to learn.

Mama wasn't ready to die just yet.

Looking back, the two years she lived with us seem strangely happy. I no longer remember the painful days, yet I know we went through them. What shimmers in my memory now are the radiant times when her spirit could still shine.

Mama's quest for a Colorado driver's license is one of my cherished memories from those days. Not understanding why she even found this necessary, I took her to the license bureau. We stood in endless lines. She must have been uncomfortable, but smiled as she got her chance to take the test. That smile soon faded, however. She'd failed!

Undaunted, she had my policeman husband tutor her in the evenings. Two weeks later, I took her back to the bureau. Mama failed again. Her shoulders sagging like those of a child with a bad report card, she said nothing more about a driver's license.

One evening several weeks later, we came home to the sweet smells of a pot roast dinner and a very clean house. I noticed that even the coffee table was uncharacteristically free of clutter. Then I saw it! A Colorado driver's license! Mama had studied all by herself. Rather than break the law, she had even taken a cab to the bureau to take the test.

We all laughed at how much she acted like my little cat, who would proudly display the day's catch on the garage step. From that day on, that license became "Mama's mousie."

I was proudest of all—proud to be her daughter. No medal could have been a greater symbol of tenacity or courage to me than that humble driver's license sitting on the coffee table.

The message of those two years was clear: persist. The broken furnaces of life can be fixed.

But even people like my mother eventually lose their struggle to live. Her breathing began to signal death the day before New Year's Eve, 1982. Bill, who had seen death only at its most violent, paced nervously around the room while the ladies from hospice talked pleasantly in the corner. As I sat on Mama's bed, reassuring her and trying to help her cross over, as the old-timers used to say, I began to realize how much this scene was like a birth.

Was I my mother's midwife? I hope so.

I've always marveled at the miracle of birth, and yet those tiny grunts and cries of life's first mystery are not its only defining event. Death intensifies life. And now that I am in the middle of my middle years, I realize life can no longer be a rehearsal for the real thing.

Mama's lessons and simple acts of courage emerge into very sharp focus.

I am my mother's egg. I am my mother's hope. She gave me life, and she showed me how to live it. Most important of all, she taught me to embrace life, to crack it open and swallow it whole.

—*Patricia McFarland*

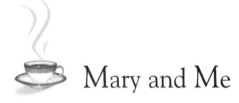

Mary and Me

Earliest Memory, 1969

I'm three and in my playpen, outside in the sun. Everything around me is painted with summer sunshine, even the dog, sprawled on the ground. I wish I had paint that color. It makes everything warm and bright. I practice looking at everything through my fringe, trying to see the sunshine stuck to it. My eyelashes have sun stuck to them, too, like the living room's lace curtains in the afternoon. Mum is busy, rushing from the back door to the outside washhouse. Chug, chug, chug—the swirly washing machine makes lots of noise. It has big rubber wringers that will eat my fingers if I put them too close. I like it here in my pen, because I'm safe and I can watch her. She smiles at me every time she walks past. Doggy wags his tail but doesn't look up. She's singing . . .

> *Fly's in the buttermilk, Shoo, shoo, shoo.*
> *Fly's in the buttermilk, Shoo, shoo, shoo.*

Fly's in the buttermilk, Shoo, shoo, shoo.
Skip to my Lou, my darlin'.

Everything is a swirl of warm sun paint and chugging and singing and her yellow flower dress, swishing around her legs. Bare arms, sandals, brown hair, laughter. If it could be a picture, this is how I would draw *happy*.

Comfort, 1996

It is nearly midnight when I arrive. The corridor is a cold black tunnel, and it is throwing my breathing and hurried footsteps back at me like stones at a condemned woman. Where is everyone? I have found my way here through a labyrinth of darkened hallways, all smelling of antiseptic and hopelessness, and I haven't seen one white coat. Room 411. My heart is too big and fills my chest like I've swallowed it. Will she see it beating? See the side of my neck bulging in double time? I know my eyes are wide and frightened. I close them and breathe deeply, trying to compose myself before I quietly open the door.

The bed has rails, to keep her safe inside. It is like a cot. I feel momentary outrage that she is in a cot. Dim light. Familiar nightgown, tangle of gray hair, proud nose, profile. Eyes closed. Chest rising and falling. My heart threatens to strangle me and pushes water out through my eyes. I strangle it back, and it subsides.

"Mum?" A gentle touch.

Her eyes open, grasp at me. Her mouth slack, grunting.

She can't speak. Oh, dear God.

"I know. I know. It's okay. You don't need to say anything." And I smile.

She grips my hand, and the inequity of it strikes me. These are the hands that held and nurtured me, that made me grow. Now they are thin, weak, and frail. One clings to me; the other, curled like a dead spider, rests on the bed. Now, my hands do the mothering. Her eyes, unblinking, are afraid. She is searching for hope in my face, for rescue, for redemption. And her eyes are apologizing, saying, "Oh, darling, I am so sorry to be this much trouble. I'll be better soon. Don't worry about me. I don't want you to worry."

She cannot hide her affliction this time. Her sickness has run ahead of her. Something invisible has happened in her brain, and it is stealing her from me. *Stroke.* That's what her hands used to do to my face. It is a different word altogether now.

I stay for as long as I can before taking my pendant from around my neck and placing it around hers, ignoring her silent protests, kissing her and promising a return first thing in the morning. She tries to press all she cannot say into me through her hand on mine. Then she lets me go.

Outside, I sink to the floor and flood the corridor with grief. I am completely alone.

Security, 1970

The big bus rumbles toward us, and I grip her hand as tightly as I can. I am in my little yellow dress and holding a white handbag. She has a big brown bag; her purse and string shopping bags are stuffed inside. Her dress is cotton and floral.

"Morning, Mary." The bus driver takes her change.

"Morning, Blossom." He gives me the little paper ticket stubs.

"Hello, Mr. Rossy." My tiny voice. Her hand on my head.

"Going to be a hot one, Mr. Ross."

"Yes. Getting the shopping done early then?"

"Oh, yes, have to on a day like this. Might be fires somewhere, do you think?"

The bus rumbles through town, and I watch the houses spin past. Her breath is peppermint-sweet as I press against her and feel her warm voice rumble through her laughing body.

The supermarket is hot when we pass through the door and freezing cold when she lifts the red meat out of the fridge. She has her hands full with a neatly written list and a basket. I stay close to her and don't touch a thing.

"Mary, is this your baby? Goodness isn't she getting big?"

"Yes, this is Margaret, our baby." I feel shy. Her hand rubs my back.

"Not in school yet?"

"No, not until next year. I have her for one more year."

"I am never going to school." I think to myself. "I'm staying at home, with Mum." They just don't understand.

We walk to the checkout, and her string bags are filled with paper sacks of flour and breakfast cereal, vegetables and tea. She pays for a slim green box of cigarettes as we leave. She lets me peel off the plastic for her. I feel happy, because I will never go to school and we will be together forever.

Love, 1996

Her room is warm and bright. The nurses are tender, mostly, although there are a few I want to slap today. Especially the one that speaks very loudly and calls her "Dear," like she is an imbecile. The television is on, suspended above the bed so she can see it when she opens her eyes. She is not asleep, but drifts in a world between dreams, awakening, and places I dare not ponder. The thin tube leaves her sleeve to find its source beneath her pillow. The morphine drips in fine pearls along it, and I watch one travel toward her vein now. All around me, people are doing their jobs. This is their workplace. I sit as impotent as I have ever been and hold her hand. I don't care if she sleeps for three days. I will stay here and hold her hand.

She stirs, and I focus immediately on her. Moments of lucidity bring her to me, and then I watch her slip away. Sometimes she talks of her own mother. But it is delirium and the morphine that speak.

"Granny. Get Granny's pills. Granny's pills." Eyes wide and wild.

I smile at her in these moments and say, "Okay, Mum. I'll do it right away." And then she rests again.

Now she turns, and her blue eyes hold me. She squeezes my hand. And it is her voice I hear this time.

"Oh, my darling."

"Hi, Mum." My voice sounds thin. I try to warm and heal her with my smile.

Her gaze is unwavering.

"I love you. Deeply. And intensely."

Inside, I crumple, but my heart beats like a butterfly. This is almost too much for me. She is my mother, my adored mother, and she is dying. Her words carve themselves into my spirit, and despite the desperate reality I am facing, I feel absurd waves of joy.

"I love you, too, Mum. With all my heart.

Everything is going to be okay."

She smiles and closes her eyes. And in the most unlikely place, in this sanitized hospital room with its inane television, pressed uniforms, and intrusive routines, something perfect has taken place, something that will live forever. A secret sacred thing, between her and me. Suddenly, the diagnoses, the doctors, the terse nurses, and the inevitability of it all are meaningless. I feel a moment of security. She has always known how to do that.

Faith, 1984

The exam is today. I drag myself through the house with lead in my stomach.

"Hi, Mum."

"Good morning, darling. I've made you some toast."

"Thanks." How will I ever swallow toast?

I am cramping. My abdomen is rejecting nourishment in favor of panic. I sip black tea with no enthusiasm and try to finish the fragment of bread that remains on the plate.

Her hand on my head. I want to cry.

"You'll be great. Just do what you can, and you'll pass with flying colors. You'll be just great." She pats me softly and returns to the kitchen. I want to cry even more now.

I leave the house still feeling her warm hug and

with the perfume of her pink lipstick on my cheek. There are no cramps now.

Her faith sustains me more than bread.

Acceptance, 1996

She is exactly as I last saw her. Her head tilted into the pillow, her nightgown across her shoulders. Hair tousled by the long weeks in bed. We are all silent, and the air is choked with our numbness. For a long time we stay like this. And then my sister touches her. With this simple act, the weeping begins. My father stands silently behind me, but I know he is crying. My sisters and I kiss her cool skin and smooth her hair. The Buddy Holly CD I bought her lilts in the background. She loved Buddy.

"He sung her to sleep," Dad says. Her longest, forever sleep.

Peace, 1996

I step up to the pulpit, my blood thudding inside me. Looking at my family, seated together in the first row, I am strengthened. The bright flowers on their lapels and their strong eyes hold me up. To my left, she lies encased in smooth wood, adorned with flowers, photographs, grandchildren's pictures, and letters. I breathe deeply and begin to speak. For ten minutes, I tell them our story.

My sister speaks, and then the grandchildren. We

all have our own stories. They place memories on her casket. Her nineteen-year-old face smiles from a photograph, dark hair in shining 1950s waves. At the end, the church where she brought me to be baptized thirty years ago is filled with applause at the joy of her memory. In tears and strength, my brother and two sisters and I bear her body outside into the sun.

Arrival, 2001

They hand him to me as I lie back on soft pillows. His blue eyes are wide open and bright, and he gazes at me. We are sobbing, my husband and I, and we touch him softly, his tiny fingers, his soft cheeks. "Hello," we weep. He is wrinkled and damp, so small, but he wants to see us, see everything. We hold each other, and in my heart I sing to him:

> *Fly's in the buttermilk, Shoo, shoo, shoo.*
> *Fly's in the buttermilk, Shoo, shoo, shoo.*
> *Fly's in the buttermilk, Shoo, shoo, shoo.*
> *Skip to my Lou, my darlin'.*

We name him Samuel. I am his mother. And she will always be his grandmother.

—Maura Bedloe

Caroline's Prince

My three-year-old daughter, Caroline, believes that people come in three categories: princesses, princes, and workhorses. Inevitably, I fall into the workhorse category, while she presides over the princess line. Hers is not a Habsburg chin or an iron fist but a natural talent to rule and to show by example. Minutes after she was born, her father carried her around the delivery room, and to everybody's astonishment, she held her head up high and looked around the room with the attitude of Queen Victoria.

A platinum-blond princess, she wears tiaras at breakfast, high heels for lunch, and ball gowns for dinner. Her six-year-old brother, who has tired of all the hoopla, has but one term for her: piece of work. Her second alias is "Cato," after her Dutch great-grandmother Catherine and her Norwegian great-grandfather Cato. But I am beginning to think that, in

Caroline's case, the name Cato is more closely related to the Roman statesman Cato, who was known for his wisdom and wit. Caroline's wisdom is the only one that counts, and anyone who dissents falls out of grace and can expect a kick in the rear, no matter that Her Royal Highness is wearing high heels.

The three workhorses (her father, her brother, and me) are hardly worthy of her. However, she, aware of her *noblesse oblige*, puts up with us as if we are a bunch of indentured but loyal and rapidly aging servants. Besides, in order for her throne to rise above her subjects, she needs losers like us to lean upon.

At three, she is conscious of the arts of affectation, grace, and elegance. Unfortunately, however, her finer sense of elocution leaves much to be desired. A booming voice may come with the territory, but when Workhorse #1 took her to the bathroom of the Chinese restaurant to pat her on her diapered regal bottom because she pitched her fork at a bald man's head in a fit of royal rage, Princess Caroline yelled so loud that the entire restaurant could hear her indignant, "How dare you hit me!"

Besides her voluminous voice, she is unabashedly uninhibited for an aristocrat. One hot afternoon she threw off all her clothes and sported her naked body in front of her mortified grandfather.

"Wanna see my kagina?" she proposed, as if she were consulting him on a flower arrangement.

Her grandfather had no desire to see any kaginas, and William, Workhorse #3, told his sister that even princesses have "*v*aginas," to which Her Majesty replied that she knew best, and then turned up her royal bottom in his direction and let out a princely pretend-fart.

By the way, Shrek is her favorite matinee idol. On her more imaginative days, she tells me that she will play Princess Fiona if I am prepared to turn green and play an ogre. But an ogre is not the Prince Charming she has been waiting for. Her prince turned up in the guise of her swim instructor this summer. Although Princess Caroline wondered why she should bother with swimming when she would one day have a royal yacht at her disposal in every harbor, when she laid eyes on Prince Kevin, she was sold on the idea of getting wet.

Kevin is, after all, a prince in every way: He is *dark* (tan like a Californian surfer) and *mysterious* (Caroline still can't "read" him; when he walks by, oblivious of Caroline's hungry looks, she tells me he is "sooooo funny!"). Furthermore, he is *young* (fourteen, maybe fifteen) and *handsome* (he beats Shrek in that department) as well as *polite* and *courteous* (even when Caroline opens her treasure trove of trivia to him, he patiently listens). Above all, since he is *strong* enough to drag all of Caroline's pudgy forty pounds through the pool, he'd be strong enough to slay her dragon, too. (Workhorse #3 would disagree here and tell me that Caroline *is* the dragon.)

All joking aside, after meeting Kevin, Caroline told me that Workhorse #2 (Daddy) would no longer do as a potential hubby. She may still consider dancing with Workhorse #2 at her wedding, but as a groom he is completely out of the picture.

Since I had never seen a three-year-old falling head over heels for a much older man, I decided to observe her tactics. It might come in handy if I were to become widowed young and needed to find myself a trophy husband with gray hair and prostate problems.

Her mating game went like this: First, there was coyness—her little (big) head would avoid any eye contact. She would look down at her toes or pretend to be counting the polka dots on what she calls her "ballerina" swimsuit (it has a little skirt in the back). I had never seen Princess Caroline so humble and civilized. But soon this kind of evasion and hiding behind the cellulite-legs of Workhorse #1 gave way to open flirtation.

This also meant that Kevin had advanced from distant prince status to outright hunk status. She bragged about Kevin's good looks and great talents as a swim instructor to Workhorse #3, who, deeply immersed in reading *Pippi Longstocking,* could not have cared less.

It also meant that I no longer had to drag her

into the water to where Kevin was sitting at the beginning of each lesson. Instead, she would bounce and skip toward him like a Playboy bunny on steroids. She'd show him how she could hop on one leg and how she could fold up her outer ear and stash it inside her ear canal. Then, unable to hear Kevin's compliments on her ear acrobatics, she'd say *"What?"* like a deaf grannie.

She relished the body contact she had with him in the pool: the way she draped her hands on his broad shoulders when practicing the breast stroke; the way his head would touch hers as she practiced the backstroke; the way she would blow bubbles with him and throw her voluptuous body at him during diving practice. She was in swim heaven, and all because of Kevin.

For years, every time we'd wash her goldilocks in the bathtub, she would scream bloody murder and tell us she was going to divorce us all. Needless to say, when Kevin asked her to put her face in the water, she went underwater with a smile on her face—heck, she'd stick her head down the toilet, if he asked.

Then came vanity. After all, with drenched hair, she was not assured of her royal good looks. In between head dunks, she would straighten up and comb back her wet hair with her fingers and pull it behind her ears, or ask Kevin whether she was having a good hair moment.

"Yes, your hair looks fine," I heard him utter several times with a boyish nonchalance in his maturing voice.

Once Kevin had seen her with wet hair, the degree of intimacy went up, and Caroline deemed it proper to move into her all-out casual mode—that is, incessantly listing all the characters in *Dragon Tales* and chatting so much about her favorite television shows that Kevin started throwing looks of desperation at me. Obviously, he wanted her to shut up and get on with the lesson. Meanwhile, she was hopping on one leg again and recounting an episode of *Powerpuff Girls*: "And 'member on the *Powerpuff Girls* when Professor Utonium . . ." The summer can be long and dreary when you do nothing but teach three-year-old girls to swim.

When Caroline ran out of her television repertoire, she became daring and began stalking Kevin all over the pool terrain. The moment she'd spot him, her face would light up and she'd think up a little plan to sneak up on him and surprise him with the forever-fascinating trivia from a day in the life of Princess Caroline.

One afternoon as she watched his wet limbs come out of the water, her scenario-planning kicked into full gear.

"What if," she told me, grabbing her pink bath

towel, "I pull this towel over my head, walk up to him, throw off the towel, and tell him my dog's name is Smokey?"

"Excellent plan, my darling," I replied. "And such an important piece of information," I whispered to Workhorse #3, who was painstakingly and prudishly covering up his six-year-old nudity with his own towel.

Off she went, a pair of chubby legs underneath a pink towel. The towel with legs was seen all over the terrain, trailing Kevin. I think Kevin was embarrassed, for he kept walking away at the pivotal moment. So, she came back, perspiring with disappointment. As she reported back to me, her glance hovered past my shoulder, and a new plan popped into her little pageboy-styled noggin.

Showing off her one dimple, she said connivingly, "Oh wait . . . he is walking to the canteen. If I go sit on the little bench over there, he'll see me when he comes out."

It was sheer genius—had Kevin not already walked away, passing behind the little bench. But Caroline hadn't noticed his departure, so she sat down on the bench, folded her hands in her lap, and waited. She sat and patted her hair, making sure it was all pretty. She sat and licked her lips—toddler lipstick. She sat and looked at her nails, regretting that the pink nail polish was wearing off and uneven.

And she waited and waited. People started noticing her, and someone finally asked, "Who are you waiting for, little girl?"

With the composure of a princess, she batted her eyelashes like Scarlett O'Hara and sighed with the passion of Miss Piggy: "Kevin."

The guy at the canteen overheard her, grabbed his mike, and called across the land: "Can Kevin come to the canteen?"

At that point I walked up to her, but as soon as she saw me approaching, she said "Shoo!" as if I was a bothersome and intrusive fly that needed to be chased out of the room. When I failed to get the hint, she yelled, "Get lost, Mom! Kevin is coming!"

For a moment I had a flashback to when I was sixteen, minding my own business on a beach in Portugal. A Portuguese Romeo with sideburns down to his jaw lay down next to me and told me that northern European women, with their blond hair and fair skin, were goddesses. My mother, witnessing all of this from her hotel-room balcony, had marched in a beeline to the beach and told me to pack up and leave.

And here I was: I had become my mother.

So, Caroline had her little rendezvous with Kevin, telling him that she had a Band-Aid on her knee, a dog named Smokey, and a mother who turned up at the most embarrassing moments.

She returned to me triumphant at having accomplished her mission—and seeming more thirteen than three. Later, I told Workhorse #2 (her dad) that we should consider hiding birth control pills in her cereal the moment she started having periods.

At bedtime, I tucked her in, brushed her soft cheek with mine, and inhaled her sweet innocence. She framed my face with her little hands, and gazing earnestly at me with clear blue eyes, she said, "I love you, Mommy." As always, it was the moment that made my day.

As I left the room and flipped off the light switch, I looked back at her little round-bellied shape on the bed and whispered, "Good night, sweet Caroline— I'm glad you've found your prince."

—*Inez Hollander Lake*

The Old Indian Woman

My mother tells a great story about an episode she had in a grocery store years ago. She was doing her weekly grocery shopping, and as she moved near the overripe tomatoes, she spied an older Indian woman across the aisle, doing her shopping. The woman had long black hair with streaks of gray and high cheekbones that were striking and made her stand out from the mass of suburban moms with sun-bleached curls. Intrigued, my mother moved closer.

At this point in her story, my mother always pauses to laugh. It took only a few steps toward the unusual woman for her to see that she had caught her own reflection in the mirror above the vegetable display.

Looking back on that story, I realize that my mother had to be in her forties when she had that chance encounter with the Indian woman in the mirror. As I draw closer to that same decade, it makes me wonder about my own reflection, but only as it compares to hers. And it is clear to me how much harder she worked and how much more in control of family life she was than I.

I was in one of these pondering moods recently, on a hot, dry June day when my mother and I traveled to an organic farm on the eastern Colorado plains to pick strawberries. I'd had an especially out-of-control week, and as we drove along the interstate and talked, I eyed her suspiciously. There was a secret to all this family organizing stuff, and she was holding back.

We reached the farm and soon were bent over the long rows, plucking the sticky, soft fruit. It took only minutes before I started wondering how long we would stay. My neck and back started to cramp in protest to the position of squatting, and the sun baked my neck. I had forgotten a hat and sunscreen.

I tried to keep quiet as my mother moved methodically, without complaint, down her row. In the shade of her straw hat, she started to hum quietly, which, quite frankly, annoyed me. I probably made it only an hour and a half before I shamelessly used my baby as an excuse to stop picking. It was, after all, almost noon, and I did need to get him home for a nap. There was no complaint from my gray-haired mother, just a nod of understanding as we wrapped up the fruit and headed for home.

We were quiet on our drive back to town as the baby slept soundly in his car seat and the engine droned. For some reason, I started thinking about my mom at my stage in life. I remembered one of her oil paintings, a partially completed masterpiece with five little faces on it. During her early childbearing years of the 1960s, she would clear a place on the large square of canvas and paint the face of each child as he or she turned two. The unfinished oil sat in our basement for years under a painter's cloth. As kids, we would go down and peek at it from time to time.

The first three children are complete, the fourth is half done, and the fifth is a murky white oval on the canvas. As the sixth child, I was not even a mark on the painting.

It occurred to me that the painting was a snapshot of my mother at my age, a visual representation of her life at the time, capturing her love of her children and the growing responsibilities that took her away from the brushes and turpentine. It had never occurred to me before, but the size of the canvas could never have held eight small faces. Had her life taken a different turn from what she had planned? Had she ever been a self-doubting, unsure mother? Did her life sometimes spin out of control? Perhaps her confidence came from trial and error, with time.

I think that is why, given that realization, I was stunned the day I found myself at an end-of-season sale in a trendy department store. Diving into the rack of rejected silky clothes, I glanced up and caught my reflection in a mirror across the aisle. It was there that I saw someone who both shocked me and gave me hope.

There stood an old Indian woman.

—*Marla Kiley*

My Declaration

In the book is an old postcard of a street facing a hotel in Cairo, with dusty Egyptians leading Britain's best-dressed tourists in horse-drawn carriages. The postcard marks page 118 of *Edna St. Vincent Millay's Selected Poems*, and a heart is scrawled in blue pen at the bottom of the page.

". . . I," the poem declares, "shall love you always. / No matter what party is in power; / No matter what temporarily expedient combination of allied / interests wins the war; / Shall love you always."

It is Millay's "Modern Declaration," and it is my mother's message to me.

When I was only a few months old, my mother once said, my infant body began to stiffen. Not from disease, not from abuse, but from a natural inclination to be private. I inherited this from my father, a kind but sometimes emotionally inexpressive person.

My mother had inherited from her father a constant hunger for hugs, kisses, and open discussion of feelings. To embrace her as a child was to hold a stuffed animal, melding itself to my body's contours.

To hold me was to snuggle a porcupine.

I grew up showing increasingly more signs of this prickly personality. I was uncomfortable expressing emotion. I was severe in my judgment of others. I was, like my father, private, loving my family and friends quietly.

All the same, Mom and I did share interests. We both loved Shakespeare. We liked to sing. We were both writers. We enjoyed movies.

Our shared tastes illustrated our differences, too. Her favorite Shakespearean play was the sappy, lovesick story *Romeo and Juliet,* while mine featured Hamlet, the silent and inactive character. Her favorite music was officially deemed "corny" in our house, where she often subjected us to such sappy tunes as *Roses Are Red.* I, on the other hand, was touched by musicals as depressing as *Les Miserables.*

She was a romance writer; I preferred to write existential plays.

Our differences complemented each other's.

I can remember countless times when my mother said she was too shy or too nervous to speak or perform in front of many people, like I did. And I felt fascinated by her ability to cry in public and to laugh out loud and to give a loved one a strong, sincere hug.

It did make her a little sad to watch me be so distant with my friends and family. Though I let people know I loved them, I could never bring myself to pour out my feelings the way my mother did. She had a liberated heart that I couldn't comprehend, and I had a guarded soul that she didn't understand.

Yet, our connection to one another grew stronger. By the time I'd reached high school, she was more than my mother. She was my best friend in the entire world.

My mom came to see me on the stage in various shows, and she'd cry at every one of them. I read her writing and smiled quietly, hoping she'd know how much her work impressed me.

Soon I was in my twenties, and my mother's fiftieth year was around the corner. A surprise party would be held. My brother and I were put in charge of minor details, while my father took care of major planning. The party was going to be wonderful fun: Her old friends were coming to town, games would be played, a DJ was scheduled, and my father had even more "fun" in mind.

"Renie? I'd like you to sing a song with Mike, if you don't mind. She'd love that."

I felt a little sick. How could I refuse to sing a song for my mother at her fiftieth birthday party? Why should it worry me?

I had performed on stage before. I liked performing. I loved to sing. My mom would love it.

And yet, I couldn't. My brother had already begun practicing. I could hear him in the other room. With every cord he strummed on his guitar, my nerves shook in time. To act out a script for a bunch of strangers in an audience that the theater lights hid from my view was easy. To sing a song for my mother in front of friends at her party was impossible. I would choke. I might cry. It would be a blatant, and worse, a public display of emotion that I simply wasn't able to handle.

I put it off.

"Renie, we've got to rehearse this song. When are you going to be free?"

I was always too busy to learn the song. But every excuse I made hurt inside. I wanted to let my mother know how much I loved her. I wanted to show everyone at the party how much she meant to me. But I couldn't.

The day before the party, I called my brother. "Mike, I'm sorry. You'll have to do the song without me. I can't sing it."

It seemed so wrong. My mother would never be afraid to tell a group of people that she loved me, but because of my overguarded emotions, I was paralyzed. Sad and regretful, I sat by myself that night, wondering what to do. How could I let my stilted personality get in the way of my mom's birthday? It was ungrateful. It was rude. Worst of all, it kept hidden my deep feelings for my mother.

I started going through some things she'd given me over the years, and cursed myself for being so distant. As I sorted trinkets and cards, books and jewelry, I found a poem in a book with a heart drawn in blue pen at the bottom. It had been a birthday gift to me from my mother years ago.

The page was marked with an old postcard that depicted a hotel from one of our favorite movies, *The English Patient*. We must have gone to see that movie a hundred times.

Sitting alone in my room, reading the poem, I smiled and started to cry. This is how much she and I love each other. This poem says everything I want to say to her.

The next day, as we prepared for the party, I told my father that I would not be singing with my brother, Mike.

"Oh, why not? That's so disappointing."

"Don't worry. I'm going to do something else."

We greeted the guests. My father brought my mom in, and she giggled out loud in surprise. While she cried and hugged her friends, I stood in the corner. She ran to me and embraced me, her tears falling on my dress.

"Happy birthday, Mom."

"Thank you so much! This is wonderful! I'm so surprised!"

She circled the room, thanking people and hugging her friends. Then the DJ began. Games were played.

My dad went to the microphone and said a few words about his wife. I started shaking. Then he introduced my brother, who proudly strode over to take over the microphone, his guitar hanging from its strap. Without so much as a single waver in his voice, Mike strummed away and played his song. My mom laughed and smiled, and cried some more. I could hardly breathe.

Then it was my turn. My body felt frozen, and I thought about changing my mind at the last minute. Nobody knows what I've got planned, I thought. I could just say, "Happy birthday, Mom," into the microphone and that could be it.

I walked across the room to where my brother was packing up his guitar and stood there, silently, staring at all the guests. I cleared my throat and adjusted the microphone, as if stalling for time would make the experience easier.

My mother watched me quietly.

"Um," I said, my voice barely a squeak. "Once, my mom gave me a poem for my birthday, and . . ." I stopped, distracted by my mother's sudden gasp as she fumbled around for tissues. The lump in my throat grew. *Don't you cry, Irene. Make it through this.*

"She gave me this poem," I started again, "by

Edna St. Vincent Millay." I cleared my throat again. "Anyway, it says what I want to say right now. So . . ."

I was stumbling over everything and about to have a nervous breakdown. This moment had become so important to me that I couldn't imagine doing anything other than messing it up. I needed to effectively express something important to me. I needed to publicly announce that my mother was the best friend a person could have. It all seemed impossible. I saw the faces of my friends and family watching me, and my throat grew very dry.

"I, having loved ever since I was a child a few things, never having wavered / in these affections; never through shyness . . . " I continued to read the poem aloud.

My mother sobbed gently while I stood on a small stage and declared, ". . . I shall love you always. / No matter what party is in power; / No matter what temporarily expedient combination of allied / interests wins the war; / Shall love you always."

When I stopped, I no longer felt terrified. I didn't shake. I wasn't cold. My eyes were wet with tears, and my skin felt warm and healthy. I felt confident. For once, I had openly declared my emotions, while my mother smiled at me from across the room, speechless.

—*Irene L. Pynn*

Pink Ribbons

To be female is to long for what makes no sense but is in every way sensible—that which satisfies the soul. Fluffy white curtains might do the trick for one woman, whereas a garden of flowers in full bloom might spell fulfillment to another. Just the thought of hiking boots and the smell of campfire coffee might soothe the woman next door, while a full-blown shopping spree takes the edge off for me. For my grandmother, Bessie Whitlock, the essence of femininity was a pink ribbon.

The firstborn of Rosa Lee and Monroe Turney Whitlock, Bessie began her womanhood when, upon her father's premature death, she entered Buckner's Orphanage at age twelve. After the loss of her husband, Bessie's mother was unable to care for her children in their own home, so she became a matron at the orphanage, washing laundry and cleaning floors in exchange for living quarters for herself and an education for her children.

Bessie had a younger sister, Myrtle, called "Monkey" because of her wiry build and spry personality. Her brother Raymond was a big rotund boy, nicknamed "Barrel" for his love of food and the body that naturally resulted from his hearty appetite. Then there was the baby brother. Born just months after their father's death, Bessie's mother could not bear the thought of calling her son by her husband's name, though it had been planned that they would. Instead, she penned her husband's initials onto the child's birth certificate, officially naming her youngest son M.T.

As the oldest of the four children, Bessie felt responsible for the welfare of her siblings. Though Buckner allowed frequent visitors' days, no one ever came to see the Whitlock children. Bessie knew that their only sense of family lay in their close relationship to one another, and she made sure that they maintained that bond through the years.

While at Buckner, the boys contented themselves with sports, good meals, and getting to stay in the same dorm together. But Bessie and her sister craved girlish things—like the gifts the other girls in Bessie's dorm received from visitors. Bessie would hide in the shadows, peeking at the dolls, crocheted collars, and satin ribbons that were the objects of any young girl's affections. She dreamed of one day having a pink ribbon for her hair.

The years passed and with them her youth, yet Bessie never owned a pink ribbon—not a single one. The longing grew into more than just a wish for a decorative sash. The pink ribbon represented her desire for the childhood she'd lost to responsibilities far beyond those she should have borne. Bessie vowed that one day she would marry and have a little girl who would always have pink ribbons for her hair.

Indeed, time brought Bessie a husband and a pink bundle of blessings. Spry and wiry like her Aunt Monkey and curious like her mother, Peggy Ruth had auburn hair that simply cried out for ribbons to hold back her untamed locks. Though money was often tight for the newly married couple, Bessie managed to put aside little sums of change for her daughter's girlish needs. She used the pink ribbon stash to buy threads for crocheting collars and embroidering dress hems. With every dress, there was a matching hair ribbon.

Just barely out of her teens, Peggy Ruth married Billy, a young man with big blue eyes and wavy blond hair, whose hint of a smile captured her heart for a lifetime. Peggy Ruth and Billy brought two little girls of their own into the world. I am one of Peggy Ruth's daughters, Bessie Whitlock's granddaughters.

As a young woman in college, I can remember checking my mailbox in the dorm hall and finding the envelope or tiny box that bore my grandmother's return address. My heart raced each time I tore open the wrappings, as I never knew what I might find. Sometimes it was a pair of earrings. One time it was an emblem she had embroidered for my new dress. Another package contained a crocheted ruffle for a pillowcase. Each mailed gift contained a newsy letter from home and a five-dollar bill with a pink ribbon attached to it with a paper clip. The specification was always the same: "Use the money for something girlish for yourself." The pink-ribbon money embodied the nurturing of my grandmother. It was her way of making sure that I had a little something extra that made me feel special, that celebrated my womanhood. Her pink-ribbon money gave me confidence that someone cared, someone believed in me.

In time, I became a mother of two girls, Katie and Nickie. When they were little, I bought Battenburg lace collars and embroidered flowers on the hems of their dresses. It seemed easier then. Now, as teenagers, my girls seem to face challenges that are greater than those that gifts of thread and lace can overcome. They need a deeper kind of support, and I realize that the value of the pink ribbon is far greater than what it may appear at first blush. It represents the most important thing I can provide for my daughters—the knowledge that they *matter*.

Nickie recently landed a part in a high school

play. When I was in high school, I would call Granny Bessie to rejoice in such triumphs. Naturally, Nickie telephoned my mother with her big news. Days later, I asked Nickie to collect the mail for me, as I was busy putting the finishing touches on dinner. I looked out the kitchen window to see her slowly walking back from the mailbox, an open letter in her hand. The look on her face could have been the mirror image of mine after a trip to the college mailboxes. In her hands was an envelope with my mother's return address. Nickie quietly read the printed sentiments on the congratulations card, along with the atta-girl words my mother had written. But it was my mother's wordless message that most touched my daughter's heart: Paper-clipped to the inside of the card was a five-dollar bill and a pink ribbon.

—*Elaine Ernst Schneider*

The Daughter of Maeve

My Aunt Mary Ann is visiting, as she does every summer. She comes to our house for a few days, giving my mother and stepfather, with whom she lives, a break. I look forward to these visits. Although she has bipolar disorder, is heavily medicated on lithium, and is seriously overweight, there is something of the truthteller in her, like me.

I think that, perhaps, if I had not been born in my generation, my memory and truthtelling ability might have landed me in a mental institution, too. There, I, too, would have undergone repeated shock therapy until my mind, like hers, would function like a twelve-year-old's, and I, too, would be dependent on my family to take me in, to feed me and care for me, for the rest of my life.

Yet, I think that I, like my aunt, would from time to time, when someone was listening, still tell the truth.

We are driving on a hot summer day: me, almost seven months' pregnant, puffy and sweating behind the wheel, and Aunt Mary Ann, squeezed under the seatbelt around her middle. Our destination: the mall, so my aunt can compulsively spend money, buy a present for everyone in the family, and then sit down and smoke two of her allotted five cigarettes of the day in a row, one after the other, one long pleasurable inhale.

"Did my mother breastfeed me?" I ask her, as we wait at the light and the car's air conditioner wheezes.

"No," she says plainly. "She didn't want to gain the weight."

"What?" I say.

"It was thought then that you had to have extra fat on you in order to breastfeed, and she didn't want to be fat, so after your birth, the doctor gave her pills to dry up her milk, and she fed you formula from a bottle."

I shake my head. "Incredible," I say, looking at the extra fifty pounds on me, the extra hundred pounds on her. "Is it really so terrible to be fat?" I say, smiling.

"I don't think so," she says.

"Neither do I," I say, feeling the baby move within my fat belly, like a bubble of joy.

I drink alcohol for the first time when I am twelve years old. Girls at my school have started keeping liquor in their lockers and drinking between classes, and these girls are popular. While I want to be popular, I am worried that alcohol will make me do poorly in school, so I wait until after school one day and drink three glasses of my mother's white wine while watching *General Hospital* on television.

It makes me feel distant, like I am watching my life from another person's body. Though the sensation is not unpleasant, it also makes me too sleepy to read, and since reading is my greatest pleasure, I do not drink again for many years.

My mother, when I am in college, marries an alcoholic. And flirts with becoming one herself.

Thin, no longer overeating as she did when she was a divorced and lonely mother supporting two girls all by herself, she turns away from her hunger for food and toward a hunger of the throat.

I am visiting her one summer when I am grown. I have graduated from college but have not yet decided what direction to take with my life. We are at the pool at her country club. Her husband, red-faced and drunk, is sleeping on a lounge chair. I am hopping up and down in the chest-high water. She is sitting on the edge of the pool and splashing her feet gently in the water while drinking a gin and tonic.

"There is nothing to look forward to," she tells me, "now that I am married."

I look at her, look at my stepfather, wonder if he has heard. If she wants him to hear.

"Before I got married again, I always had something to look forward to," she says. "If my life was bad or I was unhappy, I would tell myself, it will be better when I find a man and get married again."

I have stopped hopping. I am standing in the water, perfectly still. I am listening to what she says very carefully.

She takes a sip of her drink. "But once you're married," she says, "if you're unhappy, there's no real reason for it, nothing you can pin it on. Nothing you can do about it. Because there's nothing to look forward to anymore."

Throughout my twenties I drink, but it is never a problem. Suddenly, when I turn thirty, when I am at an age that I can remember my mother being, my throat begins its cravings.

As a newlywed, I work hard during the day, teaching many classes at adjunct pay at two different colleges, and as I drive home, I look forward to the moment I can open the refrigerator and get that first beer.

I love beer. I love the first five cold wet swallows, the bubbles in the back of my throat, the way my day begins to fade away, the happiness I feel in being distant from my body, my feelings, my life.

Is it because I have nothing to look forward to, as my mother said?

Is it because, despite everything, I still love my mother so much that I will become her before I betray her by becoming different?

I do not know the answers to these questions. I only know that before I have made a conscious decision, I am back in the kitchen, opening another beer, and drinking, alone, after my husband has gone to bed, hiding the bottles, becoming my mother, married and working and drunk and lonely, despite myself.

And then I become a mother.

My daughter is six months old when my mother and I take her to see the new fish aquarium in Charleston.

It is a two-hour drive, and I am nervous. This is the longest I've been alone with my mother in years—without my husband, without her husband, just us. No buffer.

The baby sleeps in the backseat, and my mother talks. Tells me about work. About accidents she's seen on the road. About her marriage. And I listen.

Once we are at the aquarium, my daughter wiggles in my arms at all the colors, the flashes of watery movement behind the glass. She giggles and reaches out when the large fish come slowly near. She is happy in this underworld, so like the womb, so like the inside of her mother, where she came from, where she goes when she dreams.

Her joy is my joy.

After the aquarium, the baby is tired and sleeps soundly in her stroller, so my mother and I decide to go to lunch. We choose a fancy French bistro and sit at the bar.

My mother orders red wine, and I order seltzer with lime. I eat a plate of cheese and French bread, and she picks at her salad, orders another drink.

Near the end of the lunch, somehow we start to talk about abortion. I tell her that I have been writing about it, how women can learn lessons from it, how they can be mothers, in a spiritual sense, even when they decide not to keep the baby.

I suppose it is our closeness, this time together, that makes me think I can speak in this way. Honestly. Telling her who I am.

She is enraged. She spits as she talks, her voice a low rumble, as she insults me, hard and quick, saying my mind is mush, I have no logic, I cannot think, I have no reason.

These are the lowest things that she, a philosopher by profession, can say to me, and I am stunned at her meanness, at the sudden violence of her mood. Stunned. And angry.

I lash back.

"Why don't you just have another drink?" I say.

And for a second I think she will hit me. Here, in a fancy French bistro in Charleston, sitting at the bar, two grown women, in a fistfight.

She reins in her shaking hands, turns to face me, and unleashes a torrent of pain from deep in her throat.

"I don't know what's wrong with you," she begins. "Ever since you had this baby. Maybe it's that stupid yoga teacher of yours. Or your husband," she says, undermining my ability to have discovered ideas, feelings, thoughts for myself, "But ever since you had this baby, you have no respect for me."

Her voice is rising. She is close to screaming. "This is the worst sin of all. No matter what, a child must respect its parents. Lack of respect is unforgivable," she says, and my mind is scanning memory, thinking of our history together, wondering if it is possible that she really does not know, does not remember, what kind of a childhood I have had.

She is in childhood, too, I realize, for the next thing she says is, "I am not a child anymore!"

I stare at her, and she is looking at me, but it is not me she is seeing.

"I am not a child anymore! You cannot treat me like this!"

I am wondering who she is seeing when she looks at me. Her mother?

She has always told me that I remind her of her mother. Has my becoming a mother made her confuse me with her mother? Or is she remembering the first months of her own coming into motherhood?

I do not have the answers to these questions, here, far away from my voice, my body, where I am taking refuge from her assault.

The bartender interrupts her deluge, tries to calm her down, asks her gently if she wants the check, and she says yes. And I begin to cry, silently, no sound coming from my throat, and my baby starts to wake in her stroller, and I go get her and pick her up and carry her out to the street, alone.

For a second I wonder if I should leave altogether, call my husband or take a bus home. But I think of the baby, in this heavy coastal heat, and decide it is best for her if my mother takes us home in her car.

So I go back in.

I sit next to the baby in the backseat of the car, after telling my mom it is so I can hold her bottle for her, and when she falls back asleep, I rummage though the diaper bag, find my checkbook, and start to balance it. Then I begin to write the beginnings of a poem on the register, keeping my head down so she cannot see that I am crying, without sound, as I write.

Queen Maeve was the fierce warrior of Irish legend who took husbands, fought battles, saw blood and was wounded, learned to get what she wanted, to survive, and to lash back in return.

My mother has been Queen Maeve.

I have been her daughter, Findabair, the quiet, the meek. I trusted and loved her, feared and hated her, waited all my life to be able to be grown and to marry, to have a home of my own.

But here ends the story.

For, unlike the daughter of Maeve, I did not throw myself into a river, did not end my life when the weight of my mother's anger rose from her throat and fell upon my body.

My mother calls me later, a few hours after I am home, and leaves a message of apology on the answering machine.

For days, I am shaking.

I have, as a mother, incurred the wrath I always feared as a daughter, what I stayed quiet to avoid all my life.

And I survived.

I took that body, my feet and legs, my womb, my belly, my heart, and my throat, and I saw it all anew through the lens of history. I became a mother through my own body, and I saw my mother's history with my own eyes, my own bird sight, and I survived.

More than survived.

I forgave her.

And with this forgiveness came healing. And with healing came understanding and acceptance, and great love. And so, we began anew, my mother and I, both of us now daughters *and* mothers, forever linked by an invisible thread as universal, and certain, as time.

—Cassie Premo Steele

 Great Expectations

My daughter Morgan is sixteen, sweet sixteen, and has everything going for her.
She is smart and pretty. She has two parents in the
same house who both give a damn about her. She has
her own room. She's learning to drive. She loves to
read, listen to alternative music, and write poetry.
She keeps a journal and plays the piano. She attends
a youth group. She has good friends and three
younger sisters to hang out with. She even has a dog
that loves her. She is enrolled in several honors
classes for sophomores. Her future looks bright and
sunny. Yet, she rained hard on our parade with one
simple announcement. . . .

"I'm not going to college," she tells us one day.

My husband and I—two bachelor's, a master's,
and a doctorate-in-progress degrees between us
(mostly his)—realize that our mouths are hanging

open at this unthinkable statement.

"No," she goes on, "It's not in the cards for me." Instead, she and her friends are going to move to San Diego when (if?) they finish high school, to start a rock band or be actresses or something.

"Why San Diego?" we ask.

She looks at us kindly. We are such oblivious dolts. "The beach," she enlightens us.

"What about supporting yourselves?" We've been saving for college, not a beach house in San Diego.

"I think I'd like to be a waitress," she says.

I have to sit down. I am crushed. I start doing some math aloud: "Let's see, minimum wage times forty hours a week, times four weeks, minus rent and utilities, and how much did you say a new CD costs?"

"I'll get two jobs," she says belligerently. "I'm doing this."

My husband shushes me. When Morgan goes up to her room, he smiles. "When I was sixteen," he says, "I was either going to get a VW van with my friend Robert and drive to California or join the military."

"When I was sixteen," I say, resisting comfort, "I wanted to go to college."

College was the whole point of life. I was one of "those" kids: an exemplary student, a grind, a nerd. I loved school and endured summer vacation. (I freckled easily and would rather be conjugating irregular French verbs, thank you.)

When I started high school, my parents had to sign the registration form, on which you had to specify general studies, secretarial/business, or college preparatory. I, of course, had checked the box next to college prep. My mother frowned. She showed it to my father. "Why would she check that?" she asked in all seriousness.

"Because I want to go to college," I answered.

"Why?"

"Because I do. Doesn't everyone?"

"What a waste of time," my mother said. "You change that to secretarial."

"Secretarial?" I spat out the word contemptuously.

"That's what girls do!" my mother said. "You learn to type and take shorthand, so you can get a job until you get married."

"Mom!" I shrieked. "I will never be a secretary! What a crappy life!"

"That's what I did." She sulked. "I worked for Prudential Insurance until your brother was born. I was very good at shorthand."

I was dumbfounded. She was insulted.

"Oh, let her go to college," said my indulgent dad. "She's smart. And it's a good place to meet a husband."

While my mother muttered dark predictions about my future unemployability, I became college-bound. In a way, my mother turned out to be right.

With a degree in theater, I was somewhat unemployable. I taught creative dramatics and worked for a theater company that interacted with disabled populations. But my paychecks were small enough that I also poured beer at Shakey's Pizza and cleaned bank offices at night.

My father was proven right as well: I did meet my husband in college, and we've been together ever since. We both have jobs in education, for which we thank our college degrees. And we know that the experience of college, for each of us in innumerable ways, was enlightening, formative, challenging, and integral to whom we are today.

So, the question remains, long into the hours when I am supposed to be asleep: How did we raise a child who so disregards the importance of education?

We want to blame ourselves. We haven't spent enough time with her. We've spent too much time. We didn't read enough to her. We read her too many books. We haven't monitored her friends closely enough. We've sheltered her too much. Why are her grades sinking? Why is her motivation dissipating, her interest flagging? What have we done wrong?

"School is boring," she says. "Period. I can't wait till it's over. Why would I volunteer for four more years of boring?"

Friends tell us we are panicking needlessly. (At least I am; my husband remembers the VW van.)

Maybe a year or two off will clarify her vision of her future. Maybe one truly can have a fulfilling life without college.

A friend suggests we make Morgan get a job at Subway this summer. "Give her a few months of grumpy people shoving sandwiches back at her and saying, 'I said NO LETTUCE!' Then she'll go to college for sure."

At the heart of my discomfort, is this knowledge: I have become my mother. The cycle is repeating itself, in spite of my best intentions. I, who so chafed at my mother's inflexibility and lack of understanding, am treating my daughter the exact same way. I loved school; therefore you, too, must love school. I was college-bound; therefore you must be, too. My expectations of Morgan are not her problem. They're mine. But my initial, palpable disappointment in her announcement is her problem, for I know she is translating it into my loss of love for her. That is a problem I must fix.

It's a precision dance, mothering. How do you have standards for your children and still love and accept them completely? How do you transcend your own experience as the yardstick for measuring their lives? How do you help them to grow, even as they make choices you can't stand?

"Will you be mad if I'm a lesbian?" my ten-year-old demands.

Here is a new vocabulary word, I think. I tell her I will love her no matter what, and it's so easy to mean that unconditionally when reassuring a fifth-grader who has just learned a new concept. The harder part comes later, at sweet sixteen. You still know you'll love her no matter what, but the expression gets lost as the expectations are unceremoniously dumped. I think of the choices my siblings and I have made in our lives, some better than others, and how my parents still welcome us for Christmas every year. They may not approve of us, but they love us, and we know that. That's the part of my mother that I hope comes through in me, as I try to find gentle ways to guide my oldest daughter, to accept her life decisions, and to love her in a way that she feels is sincere and unconditional.

I expected the diapers, the weaning, the menstrual period, the questions, the driver's license, the young adult. It seems I just never expected her to be different from me.

—*Valerie Schultz*

"Great Expectations" was originally published as "No College for Me!" in *Mothering* magazine, March/April 2002.

The Shoebox

All I have of my mother is her genetic code and the contents of a box. It is just a shoebox, a cheap, transparent acrylic box with a blue lid from a dollar store. It usually hides in the back of my closet, rarely seeing the light of day.

Now, I sit propped up on my bed with the shoebox that contains the highly distilled essence of my mother's life. It's not a very full shoebox, either. Georgia's life was very short. My grandmother and my aunts saved all these precious memories and handed them on to me. I turn to the box on this rainy afternoon like a crime scene investigator trying to profile my mother. The contents leave me with more questions than answers.

A fancy, leather-bound book entitled "Treasured Memories" from her funeral tells me on the first page that she was born October 29, 1935, in Ashford, West

Virginia, and died on April 7, 1956. For those who are not good at math, it even says she was twenty years old. It says nothing about all that transpired in between. It says nothing about her favorite food or her favorite color. I don't know who filled in this book, but I find it quite annoying that they didn't get it right. Aside from saying nothing about the kind of person my mother was, whoever filled it out didn't even spell the names of those involved correctly. Whether the errors were made because of profound grief or because someone who barely knew the family filled it out, I will never know. My father Hollis is "Hollie"; my name, Pamela, is "Pamila." Small stuff, I know, but I sit here forty-six years later watching the rain slide down the window, and I don't know if I should white it out and make it right or leave it alone to stand testament.

The box also contains her certificate of baptism from April 22, 1945, and I see she was still in Ashford, West Virginia. There is a yellowed report card from Sherman High School in Boone County, West Virginia, for the school year 1951–1952, her eleventh grade. There are no other report cards, and I wonder why just this one survived. Was it her last? It seems I recall hearing that she did not graduate from high school. I had always been told that my mother was very bright, but this tells a different story. Not an *A* anywhere in sight. Georgia got *D*s in history, typing, and shorthand; *C*s in English and phys ed.

The comments are interesting, too. "You squirt— you have added much pleasure to this class." It seems important to know who wrote this, but there is no clue. Another comment, scrawled diagonally in the second semester space, reads, "Georgia—Never still. Adams." I'm assuming that Adams was the teacher and that my mom was hyperactive. Well, there's the origin of one of my behaviors. I cannot sit still.

There are four letters in the box. One letter is type-written, which is curious for someone who got a *D* in typing. This letter is written to her sister-in-law, Betty, on the occasion of the announcement of Betty's pregnancy. Georgia wrote that Betty could have her maternity clothes. She also typed, "Pam is at my back trying to get hold of the typewriter keys. The little pig is into everything." I look at the date and see it was written on April 5, 1955. I was exactly one year, one month, and one day old. Geez, Mom, cut me some slack. I guess you could say I was drawn to the typewriter at a very early age and was destined to be a hyperactive writer.

The other letters are to her mother. In December of 1955, she writes about her new furniture, her Christmas tree, and her active little girl. In January 1956, she writes that I was taken to the doctor, that I weighed twenty-seven pounds and was thirty-three inches tall, and the doc predicted I'd be tall and thin like my mother. It goes on to say, "He checked her legs and said that they were alright now." All right now? What was wrong with my legs? I do have some of the boniest knees I've ever seen, but is that a medical problem?

I was almost two years old that Christmas, and according to the letter, I got a doll that I just loved, a rocking chair, a telephone, three plush toys, three slips, a sweater, a dress, a suit coat, and two pairs of panties. The slips were handmade for me by my Aunt Doris. I do not remember the doll or the rocking chair or anything from these times. But reading this letter kind of makes me feel like I was there. But wait: I was there.

Another curious thing jumps out at me as I read the letter. She usually referred to me as Pam in her letters, but at one point she writes "Pamila" with the "i" instead of the "e," and it makes me wonder. She is the one who named me; she should know how her own kid's name is spelled. Who's right here? I've been spelling it with an "e" all my life. Maybe I should start spelling it with an "i."

I wish more letters had survived through the years. The final letter in the collection is dated January 23, 1956. In that letter she really talks about me a lot. It seems that my terrible twos were pretty terrible. She says, "Pam is really getting to be a stinker, and brother, is she mean and sassy. Every time you tell her not to do something, she up and says, 'I will so do it.' She is smart as a tack and mean as a rattlesnake." I'm sure my ex-husbands say the same thing about me, and worse.

My life has been filled with questions about my mother. I live with the ghost of a person I cannot remember. Mostly, I have everyone else's memories of her.

My grandma always said, "Your mother was a beautiful lady, and you look just like her." Sometimes I could see her holding back the tears when she looked at me and saw Georgia.

When he first met Georgia, my father told his brother, Alex, that she was "something special." Alex told me, "They were good together, your mom and dad. Always having fun, the life of the party. Your mother knew how to tell a good joke."

"Oh, you're a little clotheshorse, just like your mother," I've heard from my aunt.

"You sound just like her," I've heard from another.

"You have your mother's eyes," I've heard most often. This made no sense to me as a child. My mother is dead, I remember thinking; she couldn't see. I have my own eyes. Yet, in a way they are still her eyes. Made inside her, from her, and given to me. Eyes to see my world, except that I felt compelled to try and see enough for both of us.

The photos are my favorite part of the collection. They seem to be from the three-year span when my mom and dad were together. The first thing I notice is her smile. She's always smiling. She flashes a big sincere smile, a mischievous smile, a sultry smile; but always a smile. She looks genuinely happy. There are lots of pictures of the family. There is one of Mom and me next to the Christmas tree, with me proudly holding up my new striped sweater; it must be the one she talked about in the letter.

In the bottom of the box are some clippings from the *Cleveland Plain Dealer* newspaper. I pull out her wedding announcement and another, more chilling, clipping with the headline "2 Clevelanders Killed 6 Hurt in 2-Car Crash." Also there in the bottom of the box is a photo I do not like to look at. It is a three-and-a-half-inch square black-and-white snapshot of a car, the last car she ever rode in. My mind screams, "Why?" The steering wheel is bent and the seat askew, torn loose by the head-on collision that ended my mother's life. Bad road conditions were blamed. Ice in April in Cleveland! Why? Why was my family out driving around on a night like that? What if they had stayed home? Why was my mother killed? I was on her lap, and I was uninjured. My father sat behind us and had only minor injuries. It was a time before air bags or seat belts, and she was dead. Gone, leaving a two-year-old motherless. Is the universe so random?

If there is one thing I do know, it is that life is filled with more questions than answers. My two-year-old mind could no more understand why she had to go than my grandmother's forty-two-year-old mind could. I'd felt I was a lucky child because I had a mommy up in heaven to watch over me. That's what everyone told me when I cried for her. In time, I came to feel that a mommy up in heaven was way better than an earthbound mom who was limited by time and space and expected you to pick up your toys.

It wasn't long before my father remarried and I got a new mommy. Not too long after that, on October 29, 1958, on Georgia's birthday, my brother was born. This coincidence was not spoken of in the family, and I did not know it until I was an adult. I guess it was just a little too spooky to speak of. Is the universe really so random?

I am reluctant to close up the shoebox again; I want to know more. The questions about my mother have not been answered, cannot be answered by scraps of paper. A clean, freshly washed breeze drifts into my room; the rain has ended, and I realize that I really know my mother very well. Her favorite food had to be potato chips and her favorite color had to be purple, because mine are and everyone has always told me, "You're just like your mother." I know that she has always been beside me, my personal guardian angel, watching over me, guiding me through this seemingly charmed life I have led. She taught me to never take life for granted and to live every day to the fullest, because the universe is random and life always gives you more questions than answers.

—Pamela Frost

Girly Girl

My daughter is crying. It is the final day of kindergarten—Teddy Bear Picnic Day— and fifty-two children are talking and shrieking, engaged in frantic activity. I know there are fifty-two children, because I just spent a half hour frantically stuffing hundreds of green, white, red, yellow, and orange gummy bears into fifty-two plastic bags. Now I'm helping eight five-year-olds of wildly varying ability sort their bags by color and graph the results. So few gummies, so little time, as they say. This is not great fun, but at least I'm not stuck at the Teddy Bear Sandwich Center. That mother has to carve teeny-tiny bears out of white bread and slather them with peanut butter.

My daughter is supposed to be at the Teddy Bear Coloring Center. Instead, she is tugging on my skirt, tears sliding down her tiny freckled nose. She is the only child crying, as usual. I try to swallow my impatience.

"What's wrong?" I ask.

"Cameron won't let me use the red crayon!" She sniffs. Cameron is short and funny, with a face and personality not unlike Dennis the Menace.

"Did you ask him nicely if you could borrow it?" I ask.

"Yes, and he wouldn't give it to me!"

I can see she's not going to let me off easily, so I walk her back to her table to investigate. Sure enough, Cameron is madly scribbling away with a red crayon, and as soon as he sees me, he begins puffing up his chest, mightily defending himself. He loudly explains that he's not yet done and that "she" tried to grab the crayon away from him. She screams right back that she "did not!" The other children at the table look on, perplexed, their stubby crayons poised in midair. My head is spinning.

"Use another color," I tell her. "Cameron will give you the red one when he's done, won't you, Cameron?"

Cameron is noncommittal. Then Davis, slight, cute Davis with a face the shape of a full moon, looks at my daughter and giggles. That's it. There's no hope for recovery now. She puts her head down on the table and sobs, big heaving sobs.

Instead of feeling empathy for her and feeling

angry with the blond in short pants who has driven her to tears, I feel irritated with her. Why is she so darned helpless and thin-skinned? I think harshly. So sensitive? A child who makes flower stews, plays with Polly Pockets, and keeps roly-polies from harm. Sometimes I wish she would just deck someone. Why can't she be tougher, like me?

I was the last of four children. I was also the only girl. These two facts, I believe, shaped my destiny more than anything else. People often assume that because I was the only girl and the youngest, the baby girl as it were, I was hopelessly spoiled and protected. This always makes me laugh, it being so patently absurd as to make me wonder whether they've spent any time around boys at all. Pummeled and ridiculed, yes. Spoiled, no.

Being a girl in our male-dominated household meant having the status of a slave. My brothers were the aggregate boss, a position they constantly reminded me of. "Seniority rules!" my middle brother, Bill, the particularly mean one, would proclaim, shoving me out of whatever chair I was sitting in and planting himself in it with an evil grin.

Females were, in a word, worthless—giddy, foolish, obsessed with wimpy pursuits like books, cooking, and dolls. They were especially dense when it came to appreciating the cosmic value of sports. No matter that this was in the bad old days before

Title Nine, when about the most strenuous activity girls were encouraged to engage in was paddle tennis or, at best, traditional female sports like gymnastics. I was accused of being adopted several times, because, among other obvious birth defects, I could not throw a football like my jock brothers.

Still, the worst crime in our middle-class, WASP family was to be sensitive. You could be lazy, you could be a jerk, you could even date a minority, but if you showed a quivering lip, a tear, or any sign of weakness, you were fair game. For a time my brothers could drive me to tears just by looking at me. They could make me cry even harder by calling me the s word. "Mona iiii-ss sensitive!" they'd chime. Then I'd oblige them, of course, by behaving exactly as they'd intended. I'd flee to my room in tears and fling myself on the bed, my face burning with a terrible emotion I now recognize as shame.

I figured out early on that if I was going to fit in with my family, feel a sense of belonging and power, I had one option. Though I was never going to be a boy, I could act like one. So I did.

I built forts. I skateboarded. I wore shorts under my skirts and competed on the field ruthlessly. I grew tough. As it turned out, I was not half bad at being a boy. I was stocky and coordinated like my brothers, so athletics came naturally to me. In the sixth grade, when I took first place in the girls' pentathlon competition for the entire school, I was happy that I had won, of course. But the main reason I was happy was because I'd proven myself to my brothers, shown that I was not just a girl in a training bra and pleated pastel skirts, that I was something superior.

The result of all this sex-role imitating is that I felt better, stronger, and more competent, and less vulnerable to my brothers' taunts and insults. They could even criticize my muscular calves and I wouldn't crack and break down like some sleep-deprived torture victim. I might scream that they were jerks, but that was acceptable—that was anger. My sensitive side still lurked underneath, but by then it was more of a low-key hum than a deafening roar. My emotions were under control.

Having grown up with boys, when it came time for me to have a child, I wanted desperately to have a girl—someone like me on the surface, but perhaps different under the skin. I never gave much thought as to what kind of girl she might be. Shy, outgoing, difficult, artistic, funny, smart: I honestly thought it didn't matter. I would treasure her no matter who she was, I was certain, and give her the emotional support and validation I'd never had. It was hopelessly banal, but I saw having a daughter as a chance to redeem the past. I now see that I was fooling myself: Not only did I care about my daughter's emotional makeup—I cared deeply about it.

When my daughter was born, I felt like the little girl on Christmas morning who tears open the pretty paper to at last find the present she's always wanted. I felt blessed, thrilled, grateful beyond words. I loved her madly, instantly.

"You finally got the girl you wanted," my childhood friend Theresa said knowingly.

It didn't take long for me to see the person my daughter was: wise, inquisitive, nurturing, and feminine. A girly girl who loved jewelry, dresses, Barbies, and all things pink. A child who would break her cookie in two, then hold out the bigger piece to you in her small hand.

Perhaps the quality that struck me most was how self-reliant and independent she was. By the time she was crawling and pulling herself up on the book-shelves in the family room, we could leave her with some blocks, a few squeaky toys, and board books, and she'd play by herself for hours. By the time she was two, she could speak only a handful of words, but would pick out her clothes and try to wiggle them on. And not stripes mixed with prints or clashing colors, mind you, but outfits that actually matched! After producing an earlier male child who showed no interest in personal hygiene, much less fashion, this was a revelation.

But I also observed something else about my daughter. She was as delicate as a baby bird. She not only cried, she cried easily and often. If you spoke with the slightest edge in your voice, she cried. If she fell down or got a scratch, she cried. If she woke up in the middle of the night and found herself alone, which she invariably did, since we declined to invite our kids to sleep in our bed, she cried until you picked her up, and even then she was often inconsolable. I spent the early morning hours of my fortieth birthday driving her around on the Glendale and Ventura freeways because she was sobbing, keeping everyone awake. Thank God she had a brother who adored her and was sweet with her, or she might not have lived to see preschool.

Needless to say, all this crying was a bit wearying. At first I assumed it bothered me simply because of the noise or the need to so often bandage her fragile spirit. But gradually I realized my irritation was due to something deeper and more upsetting: a reluctance to accept that she was like me, the little girl who once got so easily hurt. When I realized that, my eyes filled with tears.

Almost six, she is now most prone to being wounded by her peers. A few weeks ago, she attended her first slumber party. When I arrived to pick her up, she was playing a board game with three other girls and broke down in frustration when her friend Lucia unwittingly went ahead of her. "It was my turn! It was my turn!" she wailed, hitting her knees with her fists. "Not again!" muttered one little girl in an all-too-familiar tone as she glanced at my daughter.

The truth is, I can't bear to see my daughter going through childhood as I did, suffering from too gentle and loving a heart. The world has precious little space for people like her, and I worry I will not be able to be the patient, wise mother she needs.

"Kate loves to be responsible and helpful," wrote my daughter's insightful kindergarten teacher in her report card. "I've enjoyed watching her grow and mature. Keep encouraging her to keep her head up high."

But my daughter has no choice about who she is. And thankfully, neither do I. One afternoon a few months back, we were over at her grandparents' house. My quiet father-in-law, who is seventy-eight, was sitting on the couch watching an NBA playoff game between the Bulls and the Jazz. He has diabetes, and my husband made a remark that his father wasn't feeling particularly well that day. The next minute my daughter got up from her chair and snuggled up next to him, placing her hand protectively on his knee. "Who do you want to win, Papa?" she asked. I have rarely seen a grown man look happier.

I know I still have a long way to go. But she has softened me, too, broken through my hard outer shell. Over time, we've evolved a bedtime ritual that goes something like this: After a bath and a story, we talk for a few moments, and then she takes my face in her hands. "I always wanted to have a mother like you," she says, her large blue eyes gazing into mine. Then it's my turn.

"I always wanted to have a daughter like you," I say.

—*Mona Gable*

"Girly Girl" was first published in Salon.com (Mothers Who Think), January 21, 1999.

Between the Tears and the Truth

When I was a child, all my friends asked me the same question: "What's it like to have a mom like yours?" My answer was always the same: "What's it like not to?"

Mom was a paranoid schizophrenic and an alcoholic. As kids, my two brothers and I didn't know any fancy terms for her behavior, so we just referred to her bad times as days she joined the "wildcat club."

Childhood is filled with imagined fears, imaginary friends, and imaginary conversations, so for a while Mom's visual hallucinations and the voices she heard seemed normal to us. But when Mom saw faces on the inside of the cupboard doors and on the sheets of our beds, we knew they were all too real to her. Mom spent a lot of time opening cupboard doors and pulling back our sheets to see if the faces were still there. They always were. I remember wanting to see the faces, too.

I never did. One day, with my crayons, I drew faces on the inside of every cupboard door and on all the sheets on our beds. I felt better. Mom didn't.

Every night Mom said prayers with me and tucked me in. I was terrified of the dark, so she sat in a chair in my room until I fell asleep. I watched her sitting there, silhouetted against my night-light, until my eyes grew heavy and I slept. Sometimes I begged her to sleep with me. But in the dark, her own nightmares grew real. She'd lie awake while I pretended to sleep. Sometimes her terror became so real that she screamed, and Dad came running. Once she described a man standing behind Dad. She said he had an ax and was ready to swing it at Dad's head. I screamed, because I thought I saw it too. Dad turned on the light, and no one was there. We slept with the light on, just in case. I pretended my sheets and blankets were armor that kept us safe.

Mom was convinced that our family was being watched every minute. She believed cameras were hidden in every room. She believed the local television stations recorded every move we made, and broadcasted them on every channel. Sometimes I woke up at night and heard her crying. I would tiptoe into the living room where she sat staring at the television screen, a glass of vodka in her hand. The screen was filled with static. She cried, because what she saw there was us, our every move, even the most private ones.

We grew up loving her fiercely. We protected her.
We defended her. I think we loved her so much
because Dad loved her even more. I remember many
nights when he felt her pain. He was strong for her. He
held her and patiently explained that the faces weren't
there, the voices weren't real. He begged her to come
to bed, to go to sleep. When I was in high school I
asked him why he stayed with Mom even though life
with her was so difficult. "Because I promised I would,"
he answered. To love, to honor, to cherish, in sickness
and in health until death do us part. It was all there in
his wedding vows. "Simple," he said. "Simple."

Mom was in and out of the psychiatric hospital
five times, ninety days each time. She suffered a
major breakdown after each of us was born, another
one when I was in second grade, and her last when I
was nineteen years old. I visited her every other day
at the hospital during that last breakdown. I signed
her out of her ward, and we went for walks on the
hospital grounds. Sometimes she wouldn't talk at all.
Sometimes she cried. Sometimes she told me how
awful group therapy was. She told me the doctors
pushed the patients to talk. One day they pushed too
hard, and a woman in her group committed suicide.
Mom didn't want to stay at the hospital after that, so
each time the doctors gave her an evaluation, she
answered all the questions both true and false, and
she circled all the answers on the multiple-choice

sections. She wanted to be sure she gave them the correct answer. Ninety days is a long time.

I have many happy memories from childhood, too. I remember dew on the toes of my new red sneakers, learning to ride a two-wheeler, playing house, and playing "kick the can" on summer nights. I remember balancing on the railroad tracks, and I remember having to go home when the streetlights came on at dusk. I remember penny candy, lemonade stands, and a rabbit named Junior. When I think of Mom, I remember bedtime prayers, warm cookies, and getting a home permanent. I remember magical Christmases, special birthday meals, and a pink angora sweater.

Someone once told me that I should seek counseling to come to terms with the fact that I grew up with a dysfunctional mother. I've already come to terms with that, many times. When I say bedtime prayers with my son, or bake cookies, or make Christmas magical, I come to terms with it. I came to terms with all of it somewhere between the tears and the truth. Somehow I know Mom came to terms with it, too. I have no regrets. I place no blame. When I visit Mom's grave, I pray and I know, by the grace of God, that I loved her. Totally. Completely. Because, in my heart, I promised I would.

Simple.

—Patricia Clark

The Legacy

When I was five years old, my family moved from Edmonton, Alberta, Canada, to Berkley, California, for a year while my father worked on his graduate degree. My mother's words and actions convinced me that we were embarking on a wonderful adventure and transformed my anxiety into excitement.

Years later, as a grown woman with children of my own, I realized what she had gone through to make my father's dreams come true. She rented her lovely home to strangers, packed up what she could fit into a Volkswagen with a cartop carrier, and moved to a filthy, cockroach-infested apartment surrounded by strangers. That was when my mother taught me that sometimes you have to look past your own desires to the highest good of those you love.

We moved into old army barracks, transformed

after World War II into married students' quarters for the University of California. My mother cried when she saw the hovel masquerading as an apartment, but her sorrow and self-pity were short-lived. Within days she created a home for us, complete with curtains that she'd stayed up all night making on her sewing machine. That was when my mother taught me that it didn't matter where we lived as long as we were together.

Not long after we arrived, I started kindergarten and experienced my first bout of homesickness. My sixth birthday was only two weeks away, and I wanted a party. Trouble was, I wanted a party just like the ones I remembered from previous years—in the backyard and basement of our house in Edmonton, surrounded by my friends from the neighborhood, and not in this strange place where I felt so alone and different.

The morning of my birthday, my mother promised that we would have a special supper that night with a birthday cake for dessert and, of course, presents.

"We'll have a wonderful time," she said. "And soon, you'll have lots of new friends. We can have a party anytime. It doesn't have to be your birthday."

Despite her reassuring words, I went to school full of sadness and disappointment. Just before recess, we heard a knock at our classroom door.

"That must be our special surprise," the teacher

said and opened the door.

In walked my mother, carrying a box full of cup-cakes and party favors. The teacher announced that it was my birthday. Because I was new, she had given my mother permission to have a little party at school. Everyone sang "Happy Birthday," and we all had a wonderful time. That was the day my mother taught me that when you love someone, anything is possible.

My mother's prediction came true, and I soon had a multitude of new friends. Between each row of apartments was a huge grassy area, custom-made for every sort of game. Block parties were a regular event. Entire families gathered on warm evenings for barbe-cued hotdogs, softball, and conversation. During one of those parties, my mother asked me to go inside and get her eyeglasses. Proud to be asked to perform such an important errand, I hurried into our apartment.

My heart sank when I spotted them high atop a white metal cabinet. After a few moments' delibera-tion, I pulled a chair over to the shelves, climbed up, and standing on tiptoes, reached for the glasses. Horror replaced pride when they slipped from my hands and crashed to the floor.

Tears filled my eyes and slid down my cheeks as I scrambled down from the chair and knelt in front of the pile of shattered glass. Not wanting to cut myself, I picked up a piece of the frames and with slow, hes-itant steps went back outside to what I believed at the time was certain doom. Despite my mother's gentle, loving nature, I couldn't imagine my blunder making her anything but angry.

She looked up as I approached, and her eyes widened with alarm at the sight of my frightened, tear-stained face. "Oh, no," she said. "What happened?"

Without saying a word, I handed her the piece of her glasses. By now the trickle of tears had become a flood. When I tried to explain what had happened, my mother pulled me into a suffocating hug.

"Oh, baby," she said, "Don't cry. The glasses don't matter. Please don't be upset."

She never mentioned the incident again, but I realize now that she must have felt sick about her broken glasses. My father wasn't working, and money was scarce. Years later, she said that the fifty dollars a month we paid for rent was almost half their monthly budget. I'm sure she wondered where they would find the money for new glasses, but all I felt in her hug and heard in her words that day was love and forgiveness. That was when my mother taught me that people are more important than things.

A few days ago, my boys were wrestling. Despite my prediction that someone was going to get hurt, my oldest son's glasses sustained the only injury. He came to me struggling to maintain his composure, his eyes clouded with worry. I held the pieces in my hands and remembered the look on my mother's face that summer evening so long ago. I put the glasses down and grinned at my son.

"I think I can fix them."

His body sagged with relief, and he returned the smile. "Really?"

"Yeah, really. But do me a favor, okay?"

"Sure."

"Next time you guys decide to play World Wrestling Federation, can you take off your glasses?"

After my son returned to the family room, I stood in the kitchen, filled with an overpowering longing to tell my mother that I hadn't forgotten the lesson she'd taught me the day I'd broken her glasses. It was a small lesson, only a fragment of the enormous legacy she'd left to me when she died on July 25, 1989. A little voice in my head told me to thank her anyway. I think she heard me.

—*Susan B. Townsend*

Making Mommy Pretty

My oldest daughter stopped by today on her way to a job interview. At twenty-one, Erin was ready to venture into the corporate world, and I was so proud of her. She wanted a critique on her appearance and for me to pray with her before she went to the interview.

"You look just great," I told her, "Really nice. I'd hire you in a heartbeat."

She smiled and did a runway model turn to show the full impact of her ensemble. If the job were based on appearance alone, other candidates would have a hard time outshining her. Slim and tan, blond and beautiful, she looked healthy and confident in her interview outfit.

Her makeup, of course, was perfect. She'd invested a lot of time and patience in learning to apply her makeup just so. At first glance, you would think she was wearing no makeup at all. Being naturally blond, she had started by darkening her brows and applying mascara to show off her long lashes. She used just a hint of shadow to bring out the color of her eyes. A light brush of peachy blush accentuated her cheekbones and gave her a healthy glow. Her lipstick color was a few shades darker than her lips but looked completely natural.

It doesn't surprise me that Erin is so masterful with makeup. After all, she'd been fascinated with it since she was a chubby, flaxen-haired toddler.

When Erin was three, I became pregnant with her sister, and to my dismay, she gave up her daily naps just about the time first trimester fatigue set in. Some days, I desperately needed a nap after lunch, but I also needed to keep an eye on my active little girl. I found a happy solution when I discovered that Erin loved to "make Mommy pretty" with makeup.

As I rested in the recliner, which put me at the perfect level for Erin to reach me, she'd brush and play with my hair and practice putting makeup on me. I almost felt guilty, it felt so good to be pampered like that. As long as she was right there, touching me, I could rest—but the instant she wandered off, my internal alarm woke me right up.

One day as I dozed in the chair while Erin applied her magic, I was startled awake by our dog's barking. I got up and, looking out the window, saw the UPS truck lumbering into our driveway. Always happy to receive a delivery, I went to the door and met the brown-suited man carrying my package.

I greeted him and made small talk, as usual, while he presented the form for my signature. He kept giving me the strangest look. One minute, he seemed afraid of me, and the next, I was sure he was suppressing laughter. When he didn't participate in the normal, "Nice weather we're having," conversation, I got a little offended. One would think the employer would make certain drivers were at least courteous and had decent people skills. This guy acted like he couldn't wait to get away.

Only after he was well on his way down the road did I happen to pass by a mirror. I screamed and then broke into hysterical laughter. Erin had outdone herself.

My shoulder-length hair was all brushed to one side and fastened with every barrette we owned carefully snapped into a wild row of rainbow-colored bows and posies down the side of my head. She had also gone all out with the makeup. I had one extremely full and dark eyebrow, which started above my nose, arched over one eye, and ended on the side of my cheek near my ear. She had used two colors of lipstick, orange on the top lip and pink on the bottom— and, well, at three, Erin hadn't quite gotten the hang of coloring inside the lines. A half moon of purple shadow swooped over one eye, and a wide stripe of green adorned the other. She'd been reasonably accurate with the blush, applying two heavy red circles just beyond the corners of my mouth. I looked like the victim of a Crayola explosion.

The next time the UPS man came, I wanted to explain, but he seemed to be in a hurry. Never mind, I thought, let him think what he wants. But it was some time before I allowed Erin to "make Mommy pretty" again.

Today, I looked at the lovely young woman before me and thought, well, it was practice for a day like this. Though it wasn't based solely on her appearance, of course, she got the job—and made her mom very proud.

—*Diane Meredith Vogel*

The Sponge Bath

In the bathroom mirror I saw our reflection, mother and daughter. The smaller of us, a ninety-year-old woman, wizened and naked, stood in front of the sink. Her head, sitting on top of her prominent dowagers hump, seemed almost too big for her frail neck to support. She appeared almost embryonic, her small trunk C-shaped, arms pressed close to her body, head bent close to her chest. It was as if her body, knowing that its duty was almost done, was struggling to return to the shape in which it had entered this world.

Two months earlier during a typical Minneapolis February, my mother had been admitted to Fairview Hospital with peritonitis caused by a previously undiscovered bleeding ulcer. She underwent emergency surgery that evening. I, her only child, arrived from New York the next afternoon and found her sitting in an armchair next to her bed.

"This is my daughter," she announced to the staff. "She's a nurse, too." Then came the qualifier. "But," she continued, "She doesn't know anything. She hasn't been a nurse for twenty years."

"Glad to see you're yourself again, Mother," I said, bending to kiss her.

Mother remained in the hospital for five and a half weeks, during which she was in the intensive care unit twice. In my "un-nurse-like" way, I helped care for her. When she was critically ill, I was by her side day and night. I moistened her cracked lips with glycerin, fluffed her pillow, held and helped turn her when she was too weak to do it herself. We had not been together for that long a period of time since I was in high school. And I wondered if there had ever been a time in the past when I had felt so close to my mother. If there had been, I didn't remember it. I'd always wanted a close relationship, but it seemed like there was an invisible barrier between us that I could never knock down, no matter how hard I tried.

One evening she begged me to let her die. I didn't know what to say. There had been moments during the worst of her illness when I was tortured by the decisions I might have to make about continuing her life. Now, she was improving but asking me to allow her to stop fighting. Did she really want me to let her go—and could I?

Tearfully, I nodded my consent and tried to calm her and myself. When I left, I said good night and wondered if I had really said good-bye.

But the final word was not to be hers or mine. A week later, on the day before her ninetieth birthday, she was transferred to the Highlands Nursing Care Center. She settled in, and I returned home to my family and job. In mid-April, I came back to pack up the contents of her apartment at the Highlands, for she would not return. She had not been happy there.

Seventeen years earlier, my father had suffered a fatal heart attack, an event my mother had never quite reconciled. After his death, she had initially planned to move to New York to be closer to me. One day the phone rang, and she announced she had decided to remain in Minneapolis to be near her brothers and sisters. In a way, I must confess, I was relieved. Life with my mother had never been easy, and juggling a husband, three teenagers, a preteen, a job, PTA, Girl Scouts, and my mother was a terrifying prospect. Still, on top of the relief was layered rejection and shame. I couldn't imagine not wanting to be near my children, but then, I had no siblings. I wondered what my Minnesota relatives must think of me.

It was only during the early weeks of my mother's illness that I learned that it was my uncle who had persuaded her to stay in Minneapolis. He was afraid my mother would break up my marriage. He needn't have worried. My husband and I broke up our own marriage a few years later, long before my mother's illness.

The rushing water brought me back to the task at hand. Air bubbles scattered across the surface of the water as it filled the sink. I had helped my mother to the toilet and, when she'd finished, she had asked me to give her a sponge bath. I had become accustomed to my mother's body in the hospital. Indeed, in our life B.H. (before hospitalization), when we were alone she would show no shame in her nakedness as she readied herself for bed or walked to the bathroom before dressing. She had worn a womanly body, full breasts held upward by straight shoulders above a concave belly supported by strong legs, all balanced on small, compact feet. Now, I saw my mother's tissue-thin skin taunt over protuberant bones and bumpy veins, and I marveled at how fragile her wrapping had become.

I turned off the spigots and plunged the washcloth into the water. It covered my hand like a warm glove. Gently I washed and dried my mother's face. Age spots blended into freckles; the freckles were definitely a family trait. I picked up the soap and bathed my mother's arms. Her flesh, the color of the beginning of dawn, hung from her arms like a jacket into which she had shrunk. Her small face peered at me from under its halo of uncontrolled black fuzz. Earlier in her life, she would have looked at her hair, muttered the word "wild," and demanded an immediate appointment at the beauty parlor.

In the eye of the mirror it seemed like I was taller than my mother by two feet rather than five inches. My face stared at me from under my own blond and overly permed fuzz. I wondered if the rush to find unattainable perfection at the beauty parlor was also a genetic link. My mother hated my blond hair and never passed up the opportunity to tell me. I remembered the last time I'd visited her before she became ill. I had not seen her in three years and had never seen her new apartment. I had offered to come and help a year earlier when she'd moved, but she had insisted I was far too busy. I wasn't needed.

My mother had ushered me into the front hall, given me a kiss on the cheek and, as I passed, a tap on the rump.

"Gained some weight?" It was not really a question but a declaration.

Then she remarked, "Still blond, I see. I always liked your natural color."

Mousy brown with gray sprouts?

As she showed me around the apartment with its panoramic view of Minneapolis, she explained how the housekeepers were always disappointed that there was so little for them to do in her neat little home.

"But," she added, "I told them to take heart. You were visiting for a week. There would be plenty for them to do."

Ah, now I know the real reason I'm here!

The stark white of the nursing home bathroom walls seemed to generate coldness, and I put another towel around my mother's shoulders. I wiped her belly where I been planted for eight months before I had demanded my freedom. It was rounded and puffy, divided by the purple scar of the surgeon's knife. I gently lifted her slack breasts, the vessels that had given me my first nourishment, and dried underneath them. From the mirror her faded green eyes watched me. An embarrassed little smile played around her mouth.

What must it feel like to her to be in this position? For me, it was an act of love, something I could give, and finally, something she couldn't refuse. But for my mother . . . ?

The baby she had once cradled in her arms and sponged with warm soapy water was now doing the same for her. I thought of my daughter doing the same for me someday and, awestruck, envisioned a mural portraying generations of women with the younger women paying homage to their elders through the simple act of bathing. How I wished I could paint! I marveled at the beauty and poignancy of such a masterpiece.

I emptied the soapy water from the sink and refilled it. I put my mother's robe on her backward to keep her warmer while I bathed and powdered her back.

"I'm sorry."

I looked into the mirror. My mother's face stared earnestly into mine. Her once-bright eyes, now dulled with age and illness, were filled with tears.

"I'm sorry," she repeated. "I'm sorry that I never gave you affection. I was afraid I would spoil you."

I felt a sudden jolt, as if I had awakened from a heavy sleep in the middle of a hurricane, thunder and lightening, wind and rain whirling all around me. Then, suddenly, it was silent. The echo of the words just spoken hung like the still haze after a summer storm. I inhaled my mother's thin voice deeply into my lungs. Her words invaded my bloodstream, rushing to my heart and my brain simultaneously.

All at once it was clear. In that moment I not only saw me, the imperfect adult-child struggling, always unsuccessfully, to satisfy, I also saw my mother. I relived the countless teasing I'd received about being an only child and being spoiled. I imagined all the well-meaning advice she must have received as a new mother in the late 1930s. I envisioned my mother leaving the hospital after my birth, empty-handed, ashamed because I was underweight and she could not bring me home. I imagined her searching her soul for what she had done wrong. The "don'ts" and warnings she must have heard chanted in my head.

I saw my mother as a woman who had never allowed herself to relax in the comfort of unconditional love, for fear she would somehow harm her offspring. I saw that my mother had become entrenched in the habit of holding back emotion until it had become a way of life—until, in this moment, when eroded by illness and time, a crack in her heart had opened and true feelings had flooded forth.

Suddenly, in that long, narrow room, there appeared a rainbow. An overwhelming sense of peace filled me. At that moment, all my pain and frustration, all the years of unasked and unanswered questions mingled with the soapy water in the sink. I pushed the stopper and watched everything escape down the drain.

As I helped my mother put on her robe the correct way, I squeezed her shoulders and held her close.

"That's okay, Mom." I whispered. "You were probably right."

—Mary Karen Burke

Water Echoes

Water drips like mercury off my paddle, each shiny bead hitting the cold surface of the water below with a silver splash, sending water echoes dancing to the four flat corners of the earth. Clouds form in the distance and bump up against the blue-gray mountains that frame the edge of the sea. A light breeze, warm in front, cold as it passes, pushes our sea kayaks gently, like secrets, toward the open water of the Puget Sound.

I hope for nothing but a safe, dry first kayak experience. It is enough to sit atop the water like a gull, drifting soft as smoke across the expanse. It is enough to enjoy the bigness of it all without anything big happening.

My adventure-seeker, fifty-something mother pushes ahead with strong, swift strokes. My mother's brightness makes me want to turn back. I am more fearful than she. Mom is fuchsia; I am eggplant.

Mom is always zipping here and there, bolting, smiling, never gloomy, never pondering. She darts in her car, in her house, in shopping malls, on top of the sea. She is as fearless and as happy as any creature that does not know it should worry. She is always ready to enter any dark cave, looking for light.

The wind picks up my mother's short curls and scatters them across her forehead like shore grasses. She turns to me, a smile spread deeply across her small, square face. Her cheeks are flushed from the brisk sea air.

"The only thing I want to see in the whole world before I die is a whale up close in my sea kayak!"

I return the death wish with a half-smile and no comment. I shudder and pull on the old sweatshirt tucked between the boat and my right leg. My knees are cold and cramped, aching from pressing upward on the resin kayak. I follow my mom like a baby duckling in tow, but without the confidence that most ducklings have.

Reach, dip, push—glide. Reach, dip, push—glide. The constant rhythm of the paddle, at least, is calming.

At one time in this very body of water, this vast ocean inlet in the upper, watery reaches of Washington State, I was fearless. I loaded up dinghies with my grandfather's fishing gear and went bottom fishing, sometimes with a friend or a cousin, but mostly alone. I caught fat sole and flounder, those awkward sideways fish with bulging eyes, and hauled them to shore in buckets. Once my cousin and I caught a couple of nice sole, but our fathers weren't around to help us kill them. We lugged our bucket to the beach cottage where our great-grandmother watched us whack them with various kitchen utensils in a futile attempt to do them in. She cried. She sat in her chair and cried, and what was once just part of fishing became sickening and cruel. I stopped fishing for many years, and the more time I spent away from the water, the more content I was to simply gaze upon the sea instead of pull a catch from it.

But here I am once again. To a degree, I am drawn by my mother's fearlessness, made temporarily brave by her belief that if a big bad thing decides to get her, it is her time to be gotten. And despite the fact that I am no longer a child, I want my mother to be proud of me. And maybe I am jealous of the way she sprints through life.

In the distance, a small cluster of fishing boats circles like sea birds moving in over a school of fish.

"Look at the water," I say, lifting the flat edge of my paddle up, allowing the water to sheet over the edge. "It's full of plankton." The silvery water we entered is now thick and dark and soupy.

Mom grins, knowing what I'm getting at, that the

gray whales migrating here on their way back to Alaska for the summer thrive on plankton, which filter through giant screens at the front of their mouths.

Ahead, where the boats are gathered, we recognize the excitement of something happening—perhaps a whale sighting. Mom takes off, and I follow, fighting the urge to turn back. We are passing a small fishing village on the shore when the boats break up and begin to turn toward us. Then, fifty feet away, a fountain of shimmering rainbow spray breaks the surface. The spray is alive with the *whooooffshh* of air that comes from the whale's lungs.

My mother grows quiet. I can hear her breathing. We paddle in place, as the whale, one of the great grays migrating from Baja to Alaska, slips through the water. The animal's giant ridged back heaves out of the water just twenty feet away from us. Then the tail, as smooth and black as a shiny polished beach rock, flips up and breaks the surface. I breathe in deeply, my hands shaking. Intuitively, I know gray whales do not toy with boats or bother people, that this creature is simply headed somewhere as our paths cross. But while Mom soaks up every glorious second in that wonderful space of time and allows herself to be lifted into the universe of another creature, I use my time to imagine the beast turning on us and batting at us with that enormous tail.

What would it be like, I think, to topple in now and glide through the water on the back of the whale, or slip beneath it, staring into that intelligent eye as I go. Are we anything more than shadows to it? Does it feel my fear, seeping into the water like blood? Does it hear our excitement in the adrenaline surging through my pounding heart and into the sky? I hope not. A shadow is all I want to be, a curious shadow skimming the water like an insect.

Then, the tail disappears; the whale is gone. The water swirls, and the world begins to fold back into place.

"Come on!" Mom yells, giddy.

I hesitate, unsure of whether we should pursue.

"I don't know," I yell to her back as she takes off. "Oh, come on," she says, whipping her kayak around to face me. "You might never see this again."

That's right, I think. I may never see anything again, after the whale crushes my boat with its tail and I am thrown into the frigid water. I tap at the water with my paddle, giving mom my "you're crazy" look.

She can read my mind. "I'm not crazy. Didn't you see how amazing that was? Go back if you want. I've got to see him again." She turns and heads out.

I rock my kayak back and forth and tug on the life vest. Sea kayaks are quite sturdy, I remind myself. Even if I got thrown from the boat and knocked unconscious, I would just float to shore.

I take a deep breath and try to forget the fear, let it leach out of me through my paddle, let the water take it up and carry it away. I take off behind Mom, who is paddling furiously, and finally catch up. She spots me beside her and smiles, smacking her paddle onto the water and sending spray over my head.

"You'll be fine," she says.

"I know," I tell her, sending a paddle splash her way.

We head in the direction we think the whale is traveling, our small wakes following us through the gleaming water. We move against the wind this time, but with the current, heading out, away from shore. We hope we are gaining on the creature, but have no way of knowing when or where it will reappear, when it will spout again.

This time, we can feel the spray on our arms and our faces as the whale's back bulges upward, piercing the swelling water. I sit bobbing in my boat, in awe of the creature, scared, yes, but completely in awe. The sight of it is worth every ounce of fear. Its blackness is peppered with white barnacles. The bone-roughed surface of the animal's back parts the water. I feel alive in my own skin, the excitement pulling me apart from the fear.

The whale heads out toward the open sound, where only freighters pass at dawn and dusk, and whirlpools swirl dangerously, and freak storms spin about on the water.

"Let's keep going," I yell, my fear finally chased away by the excitement. The fishing boats have tired of watching. We are alone in our pursuit. We skip across the sea, throwing water with our paddles, as plumes from the whale's spouting part the water every few minutes. We know we can never catch up, but we cannot stop. Sweat is pouring down my face. My knees are raw.

Without warning, a cold wind jumps off the mountains and blasts into us. Dark clouds spring out of nowhere, circling and settling in, determined to storm. The water turns cold and dark. We head back to shore, and I glance over my shoulder several times as we go, but our whale has returned to the depths.

Back at the beach house, we dry off and make coffee and tell our whale tale to anyone who will listen. The water looks different now, more alive, as I sip at my steaming mug and look out at the white-capped waves frothing in the wind.

I find a beach chair on the covered porch of the family's waterfront trailer. My five-year-old son comes running through the sliding glass door onto the porch, binoculars dangling around his neck.

"A whale spout," he screams. "A whale spout! I saw a whale spout!"

I stand up and look out at the surging surf, but I see nothing.

"It was right there, by the ferry dock," he yells.

"The dock?" I ask him, unbelieving. "They don't come in that close."

"I saw it," he says. "I did."

A few minutes later, near one of the pilings supporting the ferry dock, that now-familiar white spray blasts upward, followed by the rising back and the elegant tail flip.

My son is hopping up and down on the porch, emotionally charged. "Wow!" he screams. "Did you see that?"

"You were right," I tell him, giving his shoulder a squeeze and tousling his hair.

He hugs my right leg and squeals. I link arms with Mom, who is watching with a satisfied smile. It is the look of someone content to live in the moment. We are quiet as the whale surfaces, spouts, and flips its tail one last time before slipping away for good.

—Gina M. Bacon

Things My Mother Taught Me

When I was a child, my mother taught me to smile and to be polite. She taught me not to talk too loud or laugh too hard, and to always have a breath mint in my pocket. She taught me to brush my hair before I went next door to play, to wear a pretty nightgown to the sleepover, and to wear a flowered dress to the science fair, because that's what "others" thought was appropriate. She also taught me to listen more than I talk, which I have always had trouble doing.

From my mother I learned, as a child, to place matching hand towels in the bathroom when company visits and to cash in a savings bond if that's what it takes to feed your guests. I learned that to prevent family feuds, you walked on eggshells all day on Christmas and Thanksgiving, and had the in-laws over for breakfast, the other side of the family over for lunch, and all of your teenagers' friends over for dessert.

As I grew up, my mother grew wiser. By the time I was an adult, I'd learned that when I was a child, my mother hadn't said no to other people as often as she should have.

While I'll always be heartbroken that she became a widow at the young age of forty-six, I'll always be grateful that I came to know my mother as an independent woman afterward. I watched her shed the stereotypes of a woman raised in the 1950s, and I now relish the fact that sometimes she, too, has ice cream for dinner.

From my mother I learned, as an adult, to give yourself what you want, because no one else may ever do it. I learned to laugh and laugh and laugh, because life is too difficult when you don't. I learned that if you dislike your in-laws or other family members or anyone else, you don't have to fake it, because life is too short to put on appearances and to worry about what others might think.

I learned that it's okay not to make the bed, not to iron your jeans, and to leave a pile of dishes in the sink, as long as you take time to sit on the kitchen floor and make Play-Doh snakes with your child. I learned that it's perfectly acceptable to serve your guests a bag of chips and iced tea, if that's all you have in the house.

My mother taught me, as an adult, that when a bill comes in the mail, to rip off the return stub, tuck it into the mailing envelope, and put a stamp on it right away. She taught me never to leave a load of wet laundry in the washing machine overnight in humid weather, because when you dry the clothes the next day, they'll smell like a mildewed shower curtain. She taught me how to make potato salad, manicotti, and Rice Krispies treats. She taught me how to shop on sale, and that you don't have to paint your face or dye your hair to be a beautiful woman at any age.

My mother taught me the Serenity Prayer. She taught me to listen to my inner voice. She taught me that, although she raised me in an organized religion, if I don't want to raise my children the same way, that's just fine. She taught me that when people disagree and argue, it doesn't mean they don't care about each other; it's when you stop caring and talking, even if those emotions and words hurt, that you're in trouble. My mother also taught me that people do to you only what you allow them to.

These are the lessons that have shaped my life. Although a few might seem passé or even silly with the passage of time and the wheels of change, most are timeless and universal. I now realize that all of her lessons came from her heart and were meant to guide and protect me.

Today I see my mother not just as my parent, but also as a woman in her own right, with her own lessons to learn—and, fortunately, to share with me, her daughter. So, today, my bills are always paid on time. My family comes before housekeeping, and self-satisfaction before social status. I still spend a small fortune on greeting cards. And I've replaced the breath mints with tooth-whitening gum. But I don't even own guest towels.

—*Valerie Smart*

My Worth in Camels

At an age when I truly believed one could die from embarrassment, I'd found the situation at the Miami airport to be nothing short of life-threatening.

The customs officer had spread out the entire contents of my suitcase on the inspection table as if he were a sidewalk salesman displaying his wares for the masses passing by. I felt like he was undressing me via my suitcase. Each layer of clothing that he laid on the table was more personal than the last, until finally my glaring-white training bra was placed atop the pile.

Now, I know all teens blame their parents for everything that goes wrong in their lives, but that day in Miami I had a solid case against my mother, Dot. She had passed time in the customs line telling everyone that we had brought back "twenty pounds of Colombia's number-one export." While I explained to her that coffee was not that top export, the customs officials cut open the linings of our suitcases, twisted our deodorant sticks as high as their plastic housings would allow, and aired every piece of our dirty laundry.

I was thirteen and thought that having my first bra on public display was the worst thing I would ever have to survive. But, that being my first over-seas trip with Mom, I had yet to learn what "life-threatening" really means. In the twenty years since that trip to Colombia, Mom and I have hung out with headhunters in the jungles of Borneo, bargained our freedom from raiders in the Sahara desert, swum with piranhas in the Amazon, and driven in Cairo during rush hour. During our travels, Mom has repeatedly taken me to the edge of danger before pulling me back to safety. She knew my risk-toler-ance level, which has always been far below hers. She also knew that every time we reached my breaking point, it was bumped up a little higher.

Though an altruist at heart, Mom hasn't taken me around the world and back for my benefit alone. Going to the remote corners of the earth has always been Dot's idea of a good time. And considering that she prefers the types of places that require bringing your own complete set of medical supplies, she can always use some help with the luggage.

Incidentally, those medical supplies made getting through customs all the more difficult that day in

Miami. After the customs officer finished ransacking our luggage, he tore into us. "You don't know anyone in Colombia? You didn't have business there? You were there on vacation?" he asked repeatedly. He just didn't buy Mom's explanation that we'd gone to Colombia because it was the farthest point to which we could travel on our month-long, unlimited flight ticket for the Caribbean. He looked at her as though she must be on drugs, even if he couldn't find any in her suitcase (well, none besides the penicillin).

I got used to that look early on. News of Mom's and my latest trip is typically met with the question: "Why would you want to go there?" I leave the answering to her.

"Because it's there, and I've never seen it," is her short reply for the remote locations Mom selects. By way of further explanation she tells people her wanderlust is the result of her "gypsy blood." That blood apparently skips generations, because her parents leave St. Paul only to drive three hours to the Wisconsin farm where her dad grew up. Dot started her travels in her youth, as soon as she could save up enough baby-sitting money for a bus ticket from St. Paul to Chicago. She hasn't been home for longer than four months at a time, since.

Mom was into "adventure travel" long before the term was coined and decades before it became the stuff of reality-game television shows. She eats mysterious concoctions, sleeps in rodent-infested huts, and takes the last ramshackle local bus to the most distant point off the beaten path—not to compete for a prize, but for the adventure of it.

When Mom began taking her trips, she had trouble finding someone to accompany her to the exotic destinations she loves. Even Dad, her choice of a life partner, has usually chosen not to accompany her on these excursions, having always preferred tamer and domestic travel. Ultimately, finding a suitable traveling companion became so difficult that Mom had to breed her own.

I'll admit I was a reluctant companion at first. Returning to school after spring and summer breaks, I would listen enviously to the other kids recounting their vacations. My trips with Mom didn't qualify as "vacations." A "vacation" is something you come back from tanned, fattened up, and relaxed. I returned from our expeditions dirty, ten pounds lighter, and kissing the first available piece of American soil.

But as I've gotten older I've come to appreciate the experiences I brought home with me from those early trips. While most kids were playing Frisbee on the beach or riding horses at a dude ranch, I was in the jungle learning to blow darts, or riding a camel by the pyramids. In addition to my experiences, I also brought home a renewed sense of appreciation for things that most Americans take for granted—like clear, running water.

The absence of potable water seems to be one of Mom's requirements for a destination. Also, if a locale isn't on the Centers for Disease Control's list of places that require vaccinations, she probably isn't interested in going there. But despite indications to the contrary, Mom doesn't pick her destinations according to their level of danger or inconvenience. Her approach is simple: she wants to go everywhere. In her sewing room is a map of the world with sticky notes marking the places she's been and the going airfare to the places she hasn't.

With a whole world to see, it can be difficult to narrow it down to specific trips. Mom and I have never resorted to throwing darts at her map, but we've come close. In the summer of 1996, we had to cancel our scheduled trip to Mali when warring tribes began shooting at tourists. Left with overseas plane tickets that needed to be used within a tightly restricted time period, we sat down to discuss our options. I began flipping backward through an illustrated atlas that Mom had opened to Mali. I hadn't flipped far when photos of the beautiful scenery of Malaysia stopped me. A jungle! There's nothing we love more than a good jungle. When I read aloud to her that much of the indigenous culture was intact, Malaysia it was. It turned out to be one of our most memorable trips. Soon, Mom and I were sipping rice wine with recently retired head-hunters in the middle of a dense tropical forest.

Mom is always looking for new places to go—not only to see something new, but also to learn something new. Mom's trips are so educational that I never had a problem getting out of school to go on them. She conducts a trip like it's a fact-finding mission for an exhaustive study of the cultures of the world. Her favorite pastime on the road (or, in most cases, off the road) is to have conversations with the locals, which, to her daughter the journalist, sound a lot like interviews.

In Malaysia she asked a headhunter about the motivations behind the practice. She learned that there is no pride in taking a woman's head—a piece of information I found comforting from my spot under a bag of skulls hanging from the longhouse rafters. In Kenya, when Mom found out that the driver of our safari bus had four wives, she asked if they each had four husbands. His response was so animated that his hands were off the wheel for the better part of fifteen minutes. Mom was then relegated to the back of the rig for the rest of the safari. While we were waiting for a bus at Ayers Rock in Australia, she talked to a group of Aborigines about what changes they thought might improve their quality of life. She gained some interesting insights, quite a feat considering that she didn't speak their language and they didn't speak ours.

Of course, mere talk, even if it does include a

rather active form of sign language, isn't enough to satisfy Mom's thirst for knowledge. A woman of action,
she prefers to learn from experience. She's eaten mystery meat in Africa because it's what the locals like,
bushwhacked through the jungles of Borneo, and mas-
tered the samba in Brazil (she was so successful they
called her "Samba Mama"). Sometimes the situation
called for me to be brought in as a glorified guinea pig.

Such was the case in Mali (we went as soon as
the shooting stopped), when she wanted to find out
the going rate, in camels, for an unmarried American
woman.

We were in the middle of the Sahara, having left
the road behind two days before in search of ele-
phants, when a band of Tuaregs, a tribe notorious for
its raiding activities, pulled us over by waving semi-
automatic weapons in our direction (always an effective method). We stopped, they took our passports,
and the negotiations on the size of their bribe began.
A couple of minutes into it, I realized that Mr. Chief
Tuareg was trying to include me in the deal—and he
had the machine gun.

I was trying to remember the smoke signal for
"help" from my Girl Scout days, when I noticed Mom
getting out of the Jeep. Mom, who always loves a
good negotiation (which is how I left Zimbabwe with
no toothpaste or shoelaces but with a lot of nice
handwoven baskets), was in her element. I watched

her, the brightly patterned standout in a sea of cam-
ouflage, waving her hands through the language barrier and gesturing toward me. I began to fill with
pride in my mom's ability to relate to people on their
own turf, in their own terms—and then I remembered that it was me they were bargaining for.

She strode triumphantly back to the Jeep and
announced, "Two-fifty."

In response to the puzzled look on my face, she
said, "That's how many camels I could get for you.
Don't you think that's a good thing to know?"

Mom had trouble believing that I'd have been
happy to live my whole life not knowing my worth in
camels. I'll admit, in retrospect, that it's an interesting tidbit to know about oneself.

In fact, the passage of time has made me grateful
for all the knowledge and experiences I've gained
from traveling with Mom. I credit our trips for my
strong sense of self-reliance. When things go wrong
in my life, I just think to myself, "Hey, I can handle
this situation. I speak the language, and there's running water available."

So, thanks, Mom—for expanding my horizons,
for helping me build the self-confidence that comes
from pushing one's limits, and for not trading me for
250 camels.

—Chryss Cada

 # Tea for Two

I slammed the front door so hard the teacups rattled in the cupboard as I took off running down the street. It was my final year of high school, and I had just finished—or at least left—yet another argument with my mother.

A certain degree of teenage angst and parental conflict is to be expected, but they were excessive for me at that time. A recent diagnosis of mononucleosis and its accompanying symptoms and medications had robbed me of my final high school track season, made joining a college cross-country team doubtful, and resulted in a bout of depression that was temporary but dangerous, as the experimental cut marks on my wrists attested.

Now, having been recently grounded for an infraction of my curfew and deprived of my car keys, I was subjected to the further indignity of making my hasty flight on foot. While I ran from the house my once-fit legs, made hopelessly sluggish by the virus, refused to respond. I slowed to a walk and finally collapsed in a park near my home, utterly drained and frustrated.

Like most teenagers—but especially so as the virus attacked not only my body, but my entire well-being—I could see no farther than the hopelessness of the present. I was especially hurt that my mother, whom I had always looked up to with admiration, seemed to have become my enemy. We no longer talked with each other; we shouted. And I found myself saying terrible things to her that I regretted even as they left my mouth.

It had not always been that way. As I lay on the grass in the park, the rattling of the teacups when I'd slammed the door echoed in my mind, bringing back memories of a special day almost ten years earlier. . . .

Delicate china and ornate silver gleamed atop the lace-covered linen tablecloth at my grandmother's house. Gingerly, I sat down at the table with all the eight-year-old dignity I could muster, my scabbed-over knees protruding beneath the unaccustomed skirt. My grandmother had assembled all the women of the family—her daughters, sons' wives, and granddaughters—so that she could distribute some of her antique teacup collection to us. Though

my scarred legs attested to my usual tomboy tenden-
cies, I felt deeply privileged to participate in a multi-
generational "women-only" event.

For as long as I could remember, my mother was
never without a cup of tea, whether she was steeping
a warm cup on a Saturday morning or rushing to fill a
Thermos for her day at work. Often, she could be
found tucked away in a corner of the house, stealing a
quiet moment with a cup of tea and her Bible, her
head bowed in meditation and prayer. Whenever I
saw her like that, I knew that her prayers for her
family—and for me, her only daughter—were
ascending along with the fragrant steam from her cup.

With trembling excitement, I selected my china
cup from the assortment on my grandmother's table:
a fine, thin, white teacup entwined with flowers. My
mother chose one decorated with the imprint of an
old-fashioned gentlewoman dressed all in pink, with
a sweeping flounced dress and a ruffled parasol to
match. In old-script cursive, the cup proclaimed her
name to be Pinkie. We carefully transported these
treasures home.

While many mothers would have immediately
put such a fine, breakable object out of an eight-
year-old tomboy's rambunctious reach for a few
years, my mother never even considered it. Instead,
she initiated me into her rite of tea. From that day
on, Pinkie and my own teacup were privy to the

many conversations we had over countless cups of tea. (For me, the tea was a weak herbal brew at first; for my mother, it was unfailingly Lipton regular with a dash of sugar.)

As I remembered all this, weeping and alone, my face pressed into the muddy, thick moss beneath the tree in the park, I wondered how on earth we had gotten from there to here. Now, instead of sharing the problem with my mother over a cup of tea at the kitchen table, my problem was my relationship with my mother. I still often saw my mother drinking a cup of tea, but she no longer asked me to join her, and I did not offer. I had noticed, however, that lately she had been drinking her tea from a mug rather than from Pinkie. My teacup was likewise gathering dust in the cupboard.

Eventually, I slowly and painfully made my way home to a silent, uneasy truce. As my eighteenth birthday and impending departure for college approached, communications between my mother and me remained at the bare minimum, with tension palpable just below the surface of each exchange.

My birthday dawned on an ordinary Sunday. In my haze of confusion and depression, the day meant little to me and was passing unremarkably. In fact, I'd spent the morning in my bedroom behind a closed door, catching up on homework assignments. In the early afternoon, I answered the doorbell to find my grandmother, wearing one of her best outfits and carrying a huge box, smiling and saying, "Happy birthday!" Wondering why she was so dressed up, I invited her in. My mother exchanged a conspiratorial smile with my grandmother, and told me to go up to my room and change into something nice.

When I was allowed back downstairs a while later, the house had been transformed with flowers, lacy tablecloths, and china into an elegant tearoom. Then the doorbell began to ring as guests arrived. With the help of my grandmother, my mother had planned a surprise birthday party for me! She had been staying up late and getting up early to secretly bake intricate tea cookies and cakes. She had invited all of my girlfriends and their mothers. She had even invited my English teacher—a favorite with all the students—to come and to bring select readings about mothers and daughters. Despite the angry words that had been exchanged over the past several months and the uneasy state of our relationship, which to me had seemed headed toward an irreparable break, she had planned and labored over a lovely mother-daughter tea party! And when I sat down next to my mother at the places she had set for us, I was truly overwhelmed: side by side once again, poised for conversation as of old, were "Pinkie" and my flowered cup.

Of course, the rocky patches in our relationship

did not suddenly end, but the tea party marked a definite turning point. Shortly after, I left for college.

While studying in Europe, I had ample time and distance to reflect on all that had happened the year before, and I wanted to find some way to convey to my mother what her unfailing love, communicated through that tea party, meant to me. As I strolled in England one day, inspiration struck, and I made an impulsive purchase. Later, I carefully carried the package on the plane home and breathed a sigh of relief when the treasures emerged unbroken as my mother unwrapped them—two delicately patterned Wedgwood teacups. "They're for us," I said, and my mother's eyes told me that I needed to explain no further. Whether we were in the same room or miles apart, we would once again be together as we sipped tea from those cups.

Now, years after and states apart from my mother, when I enjoy tea from one of the cups she gave me as a wedding present, I know that she, too, is thinking of me as she enjoys hers. I know that every day she still bows her head over that cup in prayer for her only daughter. And I look forward to the day when I, too, have a daughter, so that together my mother and I can introduce her to our soothing, healing rite of tea.

—R. M. Conner

Tell Your Story in the Next *Cup of Comfort*!

We hope you have enjoyed *A Cup of Comfort for Mothers & Daughters* and that you will share it with your mother, your daughter, your grandmother, and all the mothers and daughters you know.

You won't want to miss our next heartwarming volumes, *A Cup of Comfort for Sisters* and *A Cup of Comfort Devotional*. Look for these new books in your favorite bookstores soon!

We're brewing up lots of other *Cup of Comfort* books and *Cup of Comfort* cookbooks, each filled to the brim with true stories that will touch your heart and soothe your soul. The inspiring tales included in these collections are written by everyday men and women, and we would love to include one of your stories in an upcoming edition of *A Cup of Comfort*.

Do you have a powerful story about an experience that dramatically changed or enhanced your life? A compelling story that can stir our emotions, make us think, and bring us hope? An inspiring story that reveals lessons of humility within a vividly told tale? Tell us your story!

Each *Cup of Comfort* contributor will receive a monetary fee, author credit, and a complimentary copy of the book. Just e-mail your submission of 1,000 to 2,000 words (one story per e-mail; no attachments, please) to:

cupofcomfort@adamsmedia.com

Or, if e-mail is unavailable to you, send it to:

A Cup of Comfort
Adams Media Corporation
57 Littlefield Street
Avon, Massachusetts 02322

You can submit as many stories as you'd like, for whichever volumes you'd like. Make sure to include your name, address, and other contact information and indicate for which volume you'd like your story to be considered. We also welcome your suggestions or stories for new *Cup of Comfort* themes.

For more information, please visit our Web site: *www.cupofcomfort.com.*

We look forward to sharing many more soothing *Cups of Comfort* with you!

Contributors

Pamela K. Amlung ("A Mother's Arms") lives in Cincinnati, Ohio, with her husband and three daughters. A part-time estate-planning attorney, she also home-schools her children, writes stories and poetry, and recently served as the poetry editor for *Fruit of the Vine* (Vineyard Community Church, Cincinnati).

Maureen Anderson ("Lessons from a Four-Year-Old"), of Detroit Lakes, Minnesota, hosts the syndicated radio program "The Career Clinic," which is broadcast worldwide. She is also the coauthor, with Dick Beardsley, of *Staying the Course: A Runner's Toughest Race.*

Gina M. Bacon ("Water Echoes") works as a freelance writer, poet, and essayist. She began writing at an early age, inspired by her great-grandmother, Ruth Bancroft, a high-school dropout who enrolled in college in the 1970s and went on to complete a novel and publish newspaper articles. She resides in Southwest Washington with her husband and two sons.

B. J. Bateman ("The Comforter") shares an A-frame in Gresham, Oregon, with her newly retired husband. Since her own retirement, B. J. has focused primarily on her family, dancing, and writing. She has published several pieces, both fiction and nonfiction, won two writing awards, and completed a novel.

Maura Bedloe ("Mary and Me") lives in a tiny seaside village on the southeast coast of Tasmania, Australia, with her husband, Jonathan, and two-year-old son, Samuel. She spends her time caring for her family, gardening, beach-combing, and writing.

Patty Briles ("My Mother's Hands") lives and writes in North Carolina. She and her husband are the parents of teenage daughters, who, she says, "Still kiss us goodnight, ask for our opinions, and tell their friends how funny their parents are."

Mary Karen Burke ("The Sponge Bath"), of Mohegan Lake, New York, has four children and five grandchildren. She recently retired after working twenty years as nurse/counselor in a substance-abuse program. She'd like to thank her mother and the God of Mother-hood, who sometimes turns the worst sins of motherhood into blessings.

Chryss Cada ("My Worth in Camels") is a freelance writer, a columnist, and an adjunct professor at Colorado State University. She is currently working on her first novel.

Anne Carter ("The Birthday Promise") is a freelance writer whose stories have been published in several anthologies, including A *Cup of Comfort for Women* (2002). A native New Yorker, she resides on Long Island, near her children and grandchildren.

Patricia Clark ("Between the Tears and the Truth"), a member of the Wisconsin Fellowship of Poets, lives and writes in Oshkosh, Wisconsin, where she also works as a wife, mother, and high school teaching assistant. She believes that writing is a gift and that this gift is never greater than its Giver.

R. M. Conner ("Tea for Two") lives with her husband on Long Island, New York, where she pursues her favorite addictions: writing and tea. She travels often, in person or through books.

Marla Doherty ("Grammy and the Dream Keeper") lives and dreams in Shasta County, California, with her husband, Charles, their daughter, Nina, and several pets. When she isn't writing, she loves to teach elementary school students, prowl libraries and bookstores, hike in the woods of the Sierra-Cascade mountains, and sing.

Patricia Fish ("My Funny Mother") hails from Pasadena, Maryland. An accountant by training, she now writes full-time. She published her first book, *Everything You Need to Know about Being a Woman Can Be Learned in the Garden*, in 1999.

Kristl Volk Franklin ("The Demise of Josephine") was born in Celle, Germany. Since becoming a United States citizen, she has lived in six different states but considers the South her home. She writes screenplays and has published award-winning fiction and nonfiction in the inspirational and psychological-thriller genres.

Pamela Frost ("The Shoebox") lives with her husband in Seville, Ohio. When she isn't writing, she buys houses on her credit cards, remodels them, and then rents them out. Her upcoming book *Houses of Cards* is a humorous look at her adventures in landlord land.

Mona Gable ("Girly Girl") is a writer whose articles and essays have appeared in numerous publications, including the *Los Angeles Times Magazine, Health,* the *Wall Street Journal,* and *Salon.* She lives in Los Angeles with her husband and two children.

Peggy Newland Goetz ("The Bike Trip") lives in New Hampshire with her husband and daughter. A writer by profession, she is the author of a novel and the biographical *The Adventure of Two Lifetimes.*

Christine Goold ("Dear Mom") is a college instructor and writer. Her magazine articles have appeared in numerous regional and national publications. Her two published gothic romance novels are set in her native Colorado, where she lives with her husband, Gary. Jana, her daughter, is now a theater student at the University of Evansville, Indiana.

Carrie Howard ("A Little Night Music") is a freelance writer living in the Seattle, Washington, area with her husband, Andy; stepdaughter, Allison; and two daughters, Tessa and Lily. Her essays and articles have appeared in the *Christian Science Monitor*, *Adoptive Families*, the *Seattle Times*, and many corporate publications.

Molly Hulett ("Daughter of the Bride") is a freelance writer for a variety of magazines and corporate clients. She lives with her husband along the South Carolina coast.

Jane Tod Jimenez ("Lava Love") lives with her husband in Tempe, Arizona. Appreciating the variety of life, she has had careers in real estate, accounting, and teaching. Her writing has appeared in *Marriage Partnership*, *Treasures of a Woman's Heart*, and *God's Abundance*.

Ramona John ("Leaving"), a retired judge, is the published author of two books and numerous magazine and newspaper articles. She lives with her husband, Dick, and their dog, Greta, in Crowley, Texas.

Marla Kiley ("The Old Indian Woman") holds a master's of arts degree from Colorado University, Denver. She has worked as a writer and editor, and now occasionally writes freelance articles while she stays at home with her two sons. She lives with her husband and children in Denver, Colorado.

Martha Lackritz ("Pearls") is an undergraduate student

at Brown University, where she studies comparative literature and East Asian history. Her interests include children's bilingual education, Vietnamese poetry translation, and creative nonfiction.

Inez Hollander Lake ("Caroline's Prince") lives in the San Francisco Bay Area with her husband, son, and her royal highness, Princess Caroline. When she is not checking her daughter's formalwear and invitations to royal dinners, she writes, edits, translates, teaches, and enjoys the riches of full-time motherhood.

Jaye W. Manus ("She Left a Mess Behind") is a bead artist and novelist residing in Colorado. After raising a son and a daughter, Jaye and her husband became foster parents of two teenagers. When it comes to dogs, cats, and kids, her motto is: "Hey, what's one more?"

Nancy Massand ("Time Out") is a teacher at an independent school in Queens, New York. She and her husband have raised three delightful daughters and recently added two sons-in-law to the family. Nancy's stories have appeared in numerous publications.

Sylvia E. Sheets McDonald ("What I Wanted to Tell Her") is a stay-at-home mother, freelance writer, and graduate student pursuing a master's degree in counseling. Another of her stories appeared in *A Cup of Comfort for Friends*. She and her husband, John, live in central Ohio with their three children, Evan, Seth, and Abigail.

Patricia McFarland ("Mama's Egg") recently retired after thirty years of teaching foreign languages in high schools. She loves to travel and write, and is an avid student of art and archaeology.

Sheri McGregor ("From a Mother") lives with her husband and five children in their Southern California home. She connects with other women through her articles and books, speaking engagements, and Web site (*www. motherswhodream.com*). As a hypnotherapist, she helps others change their lives through changing their thinking.

Lynn Ruth Miller ("A Mother Knows") is a storyteller, award-winning writer, and humorist. She is the author of *Starving Hearts* and *Thoughts While Walking the Dog*, a compilation of her columns from the *Pacifica Tribune*, and a regular contributor to the *Cup of Comfort* book series. She makes her home in Northern California.

Camille Moffat ("The Inheritance") lives in the South and writes from her home on a mountainside overlooking the Shenandoah Valley.

Ksenija Soster Olmer ("First Moon Rising") is a translator, poet, writer, parent educator, and devoted student of Ikebana, the Japanese art of flower arranging. Originally from Slovenija, she lives in Orinda, California, with her husband, Mirek, a Czech bridge designer, and their three daughters.

Catherine Olson ("Before the Rain Comes") grew up

in Rockford, Illinois, and now resides in Chicago. A data analyst for a legal publishing company, she also writes short stories and teaches English as a second language in her spare time.

Richelle Putnam ("The Power of a Mother's Love") works as a writing instructor and motivational speaker. She is the recipient of several writing awards, and her writing has appeared in World Wide Writers (online), *Copperfield Review, Cayuse Press,* and *Writer's Journal.*

Irene L. Pynn ("My Declaration") works as a teacher and a writer in Orlando, Florida. She has written plays for children and worked as a reporter for a small newspaper. A Florida State University graduate, she is currently studying online for her master's degree in writing from Seton Hill University, Pennsylvania. Her parents are her greatest inspiration.

Elaine Ernst Schneider ("Pink Ribbons"), of Montgomery, Alabama, is a curriculum author for Group Publishing, Inc., and the managing editor of Lesson Tutor. The author of the book *52 Children's Moments,* she has also published articles, songs, and children's stories in publications that include *Catholic Digest, FellowScript, Parenting Today's Teen, This Christian Life, HomeLearning Canada,* and *Whispers from Heaven.*

Valerie Schultz ("Great Expectations") writes from her home in Tehachapi, California. Her stories have appeared in numerous magazines and newspapers, and she is currently a contributing columnist for the *Bakersfield Californian*. She and her husband, Randy, have four daughters.

Bluma Schwarz ("The Coronation") is a semi-retired mental health counselor and freelance writer. At age sixty-nine, she published her first story in *Iowa Woman*. Her stories have since appeared in *A Cup of Comfort*, *Potpourri*, *Potomac Review*, *AIM*, and elsewhere. She resides in Florida.

Susan J. Siersma ("The Circle Plant") recently left a long career in special education to care for a family member, at which time she began to write and to play the violin. Her favorite pastimes are organic gardening, long walks with her husband, Rodger, and playing with her three grandchildren.

Valerie Smart ("Things My Mother Taught Me") is a writer who lives in western Massachusetts with her husband and their two pet ducks. She bought a house three miles down the road from her mom's home, and "wouldn't have it any other way."

Sande Smith ("To Love a Stranger") is a poet, essayist, and public relations professional living in the San Francisco Bay Area. She holds a bachelor's degree in Portuguese and Brazilian studies, and credits her love of language to her mother, who read to her the musical words of James Baldwin, Langston Hughes, and Maya Angelou.

Cassie Premo Steele ("The Daughter of Maeve" and "My Whirling Girl") is a poet and writer who divides her time between the American South and the Irish West. More of her writing on the healing of women's bodies and spirits can be found in her books *Moon Days* and *We Heal from Memory*, as well as in *SageWoman* magazine, *Aquarian Times*, *The Blessed Bee*, and Beliefnet.com.

Kelly L. Stone ("Heart Choices") is a licensed professional counselor who has worked in the field of children's mental health for more than thirteen years. She recently published a personal essay in an anthology about sisters. She lives near Atlanta, Georgia.

Annemarieke Tazelaar ("Full Circle") was born in the Netherlands and moved with her family to the United States when she was a child. After years of teaching, she now owns her own business and a bumper sticker that reads, "I'd Rather Be Writing." A contributing author of *A Cup of Comfort Cookbook*, she claims that her novel and short-story collection are "products of her 'spare' time."

Susan B. Townsend ("The Legacy") is a writer and stay-at-home mother. Transplanted from the west coast of Canada to the United States in 1997, she now makes her home on a 300-acre farm in southeastern Virginia, with her husband, five children, and several animals.

Diane Meredith Vogel ("Making Mommy Pretty") lives with her husband, her best friend, on a farm in

Michigan. She raises dogs and goats, and enjoys writing and painting. A contributor of *A Cup of Comfort*, she is currently working on a historical novel.

Karen Favo Walsh ("Fashion Amnesia") is a writer, graphic designer, electronic prepress specialist, and caregiver. She recently completed her first nonfiction book, *Alzheimer's Stories: Tales of Mismatched Outfits, Goofy Hair, and Beer for Breakfast*. She resides with her family in St. Petersburg, Florida.

About the Editor

Colleen Sell has long believed in the power of story to connect us with our inner spirits, the Higher Spirit, and one another. Her passion for storytelling was inspired by her mother, who often used stories to guide her young daughter up "fool's hill," that steep climb from adolescence to adulthood. Judging by the stories now being woven by her six-year-old granddaughter, the family legacy of mother-daughter storytelling continues.

The editor of more than fifty published books and the former editor-in-chief of *Biblio: Exploring the World of Books* magazine, Colleen Sell is also an essayist, journalist, screenwriter, and book author. In addition to the books in the *Cup of Comfort* series, her recent credits include *10-Minute Zen* (2002).

She and her husband share a century-old Victorian on forty acres, an original Oregon homestead, which they are renovating and converting to a lavender and Christmas tree farm—an experience that is providing plenty of fodder for many great stories.

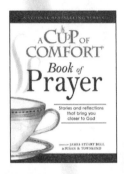